Bold Spirit
Caring for the Dying

TAMELYNDA LUX

AND 10 CARING AND COMPASSIONATE
END-OF-LIFE PRACTITIONERS

JANET BOOTH * GALE GAGNIER
TERRENCE HO * LESLEY JAMES
ASHLEE JANSEN * SHANNON KOPPENHOEFER
JANICE LOMBARDO * OLGA NIKOLAJEV
SIBY VARGHESE * CHRYSTAL WABAN

Bold Spirit Caring for the Dying

Tamelynda Lux
and 10 Caring and Compassionate
End-of-Life Practitioners

Copyright © 2021 **Bold Spirit Press**
Lux & Associates / Tamelynda Lux

All Right Reserved. No part of this publication may be reproduced, distributed, or transmitted in any form or by any means, including but not limited to photocopying, recording, or other electronic or mechanical methods without the prior written permission from the lead author, Tamelynda Lux, except in the case of brief quotations embodied in critical reviews and certain noncommercial uses permitted by copyright law.

Neither the author nor co-authors nor the publisher can be held responsible for any loss, claim, or damage arising out of the use, or misuse, of the suggestions made, the failure to take medical advice, or for any material on third-party websites.

The stories in this book are all true, but to ensure anonymity and protect privacy, some identifying names have been changed. Details that are specific to a client, patient, or loved one may have been altered as well. Permissions have been obtained for those stories where identifying names and details have not been changed.

First Printing: 2021
Bold Spirit Press
Copyright © 2021 Tamelynda Lux / Lux & Associates
All rights reserved.
ISBN Print Book: 978-0-9940927-5-5

WHAT OTHERS ARE SAYING

"*Bold Spirit Caring for the Dying* is a fruitful marriage of actual end-of-life caregiving experiences with vulnerable and compassionate demonstrations on how to be in the moment with people who are actively dying. This is an illuminating and practical guide for both new and seasoned caregivers that offers invaluable insights into the real workings of giving care to people at the end of life."

Roger Moore, Marriage and Family Counsellor, Certified Counsellor and Registered Hypnotherapist, Author

"*Bold Spirit* is a treasure and a remarkable effort which is more than a practical resource about end-of-life care. Tamelynda Lux has given us one of those rare books with the power to inspire the best in all of us. I urge anyone who is caring for the dying or who knows someone involved in such caring work to read this book. The depth of the writing repeatedly informs and inspires us to learn more about our capacity to serve others. I highly recommend *Bold Spirit* as an important guide to understanding that even at life's end, the welfare of everyone begins and ends with the caring of mind, body, and spirit."

Charles Garfield, Ph.D., Author of *Life's Last Gift: Giving and Receiving Peace When a Loved One is Dying* and *Our Wisdom Years: Growing Older With Joy, Fulfillment, Resilience, and No Regrets*

"Fascinating and profound, this collection of jewels is thoughtfully organized into a quintessential guide to enable all of us—professionals and lay people alike—to learn how to understand and to deal with the most imposing experience of life—death, dying, and grieving. This collection of treasures draws from the vast array of its authors and provides a myriad of self-care tips, strategies, and resources for caregivers and professionals."

Jayne M. Wesler, Attorney, LCSW, Author, Life Coach, Family Caregiver

"Each author offers a different perspective of end-of-life care, all of which are very helpful. Their stories remind you how unique the dying process can be for everyone involved; from the patient, to those who will be saying goodbye. This is a great guidebook, with wonderful resources for anyone who will be providing care to someone who is dying."

  Gabrielle Elise Jimenez, Hospice Nurse, End-of-Life Doula and End-of-Life Doula Coach/Educator, Author of *At the Bedside, The Hospice Heart*, and *Soft Landing*

"Olga offers tender, vulnerable sharing of her life and death experiences in a way that opens the door for us to gently visit our own. We feel safely supported to explore how death can be our teacher, to more fully live and embrace life every single day."

  Denise Seguin Horth, End-of-Life Educator, End-of-Life Doula, Speaker

"Textbook learning is admittedly important. What elevates that way of learning to a powerful level is adding the personal to it. This book offers helping professionals and caregivers an inside intimate look at end-of-life care. Gale Gagnier's chapter is a tender, honest, loving, and professional window on what is always a unique and emotionally complex process. Real-life well told with its provocative, instructive power."

  Karen (Warren-Severson) Franchot, MEd, NCC, Mental Health Professional, Author, Presenter (Retired)

DEDICATION

To caregivers who spend their lives serving others.

You are valued.

CONTENTS

Introduction

1	Death Lessons for Life – Olga Nikolajev	1
2	Grounded in Culture – Chrystal Waban	25
3	Putting on the Brakes – Shannon Koppenhoefer	45
4	Serenity and Mindfulness – Lesley James	59
5	My Boat Has Arrived – Siby Varghese	87
6	Using My Voice – Janice Lombardo	111
7	Bullshit! Yes, I Cry – Gale Gagnier	137
8	What's Up With Death Anxiety? – Ashlee Jansen	155
9	Uncharted Territory – Terrence Ho	175
10	Courageous Planning – Tamelynda Lux	191
11	A Moment of Truth – Janet Booth	211
	The Needs of the Dying – David Kessler	229
	More Books Recommended	231
	Co-Authors Contact Information	236
	A Final Note	239
	More About This Book	241
	Bold Spirit Press	243

CO-AUTHORS

Janet Booth
MA, RN, NC-BC
Janet has worked as a Nurse for many years at the intersection of quality of life and end of life, as a Hospice/Palliative Care Nurse, an End-of-Life coach, and Educator. She serves as faculty for the Conscious Dying Institute and the Integrative Nurse Coach Academy and gives classes and workshops around the country on topics related to opening up the cultural conversation about death, dying, and grief. She is the author of *Re-Imagining the End-of-Life: Self-Development & Reflective Practices for Nurse Coaches*, which was chosen as one of the American Journal of Nursing's "Best Books of the Year" for 2019.

Janice Lombardo
CEOLD
Janice has over twenty years of experience as a Medical Advocate, caregiver, and cancer survivor. She has and continues to lovingly provide physical, psychological, and psychosocial holistic support to those in transition and their loved ones. She became a certified end-of-life doula in April 2020. Since 2007 Janice has provided both patient and caregiver perspectives to help improve hospital systems and protocols for relationship-based and patient-centered care as a volunteer on the Patient and Family Partnership Council, Acute Care, Cleveland Medical Center, University Hospital's main campus, in Cleveland, Ohio. She is a member of INELDA, the International End of Life Doula Association. Janice is a certified SAGECare (Senior Action in a Gay Environment) Advocate, offering her end-of-life doula guidance and support to the LGBT community, seniors, and their loved ones.

Gale Gagnier
(nee Reynolds McKie)
RN (retired)
Gale is a Registered Nurse (graduate of Toronto Western Hospital). Gale has had a wide-spanning career in psychiatry, industrial health and a founding partner in a consulting company called BodyLogic Health Management. Upon her retirement from consulting work, she became the Director of Koochiching County Volunteer Hospice. Gale is a Certified Death Doula and an active member of NEDA (National End of Life Doula Alliance). Gale continues to speak on death and dying and the role of Death Doula and Hospice support at her local community college and community forums.

Tamelynda Lux
CCH, PCC, DipAdEd
With over 30 years of experience, Tamelynda has invested her career in supporting individuals as a life coach and then evolved her private practice to include hypnosis for life issues and concerns, end-of-life support, and grief coaching. Certified in the specialty of End-of-Life Hypnosis and as an End-of-Life Doula, Tamelynda provides non-medical, holistic support to the dying person and/or their family. She is a Certified End-of-Life Doula, Certified Psychological First Aid (Instructor Level) Canadian Red Cross, and has completed Certified Mental Health First Aid with the Canadian Mental Health Association. Tamelynda is actively involved with the aging population, including as a community member on the board of a non-profit for Alzheimers, dementia and long-term care.

Terrence Ho
Terrence is a son, brother, and caregiver. He has held roles in the public, private and non-profit sectors, where he has learned to advocate tirelessly for the greater good strategist, facilitator, and community builder. One of his biggest influences is his younger brother, who lives with Duchenne Muscular Dystrophy. Caring for his brother for almost thirty years has helped Terrence appreciate the unique needs of patients and their caregivers.

Olga Nikolajev
RN, MA, CT, CE
Olga is an End-of-Life Nurse Educator certified in the field of thanatology. Olga has a Master's degree in Religion and Culture, several multidisciplinary certificates, including a certificate in cannabis science from McMaster University. Olga facilitates Thanatology and End-of-Life Doula courses across Canada and provides support as a Grief Counsellor to formal and informal caregivers. She has provided educational presentations and facilitated many workshops over the last ten years in death and grief literacy. In addition, Olga is guiding the work of the Death Doula Ontario Network, which she founded in 2020.

Lesley James
(née Mogg)
Licensed Willow EOL Educator™
Lesley is a compassionate End-of-Life Planner, Educator, and Founder of Last Wishes Consulting. In 2020, Lesley became an End-of-Life Doula and completed courses in hospice, palliative care, advance care planning, legacy, green burials, death, dying, grief and bereavement. Lesley works and volunteers in the bereavement sector and is currently a regional co-representative at the Bereavement Ontario Network, supporting the Simcoe-York-Dufferin regions. A Jamaican-born Canadian, she is grateful for the support of her loving family and is an ally to the disability community. She is an active member of several networks and associations, which can be found on her website. In 2021, Lesley completed courses in funeral pre-planning and brings comfort and peace of mind to end-of-life conversations.

Siby Mathew Varghese
PSW
Siby was born in India and immigrated to Canada in 2019. He uses his knowledge and research skills from his Master's in Zoology to bring his passion for science to caring for people. Siby has worked on Bio-research projects in the Health sector, completed his Personal Support Worker training in Long Term Care and Retirement Residence, and currently works in Home Health Care. He lives in Toronto with his wife and baby girl. Siby believes God called him to become a compassionate caregiver.

Ashlee Jansen
BSc. Psych
Ashlee was born and raised in Nova Scotia, Canada, and she has recently moved back home to connect to loved ones and the death work community. She grew up thinking about the complexities of life, which inevitably brought her to be curious about death. Ashlee supports others with death anxiety after going through her own death acceptance journey.

Chrystal Wàban
Chrystal Wàban is a Pikwakanagan First Nation matriarch, wife, Indigenous Counselor, Spiritual Practitioner, and Entrepreneur. Utilizing decades of lived and grassroots work experiences with cultural education, decolonization, and Indigenization, Chrystal operates a social enterprise and community practice known as Blackbird Medicines and the Indigenous Death Doula Collective.

Shannon Koppenhoefer
Shannon is a twenty-one-year veteran Paramedic, an Advanced Care Paramedic who is passionate about expanding the role paramedics have in the healthcare system, specifically in the pre-hospital scene. As a Community Paramedic, she helps improve healthcare system navigation by connecting 911 callers to appropriate social and health services, providing vaccinations at community clinics, and working with vulnerable, at-risk, or chronically ill residents to decrease their reliance on the 911 system.

Shannon has been recognized by her peers twice for her dedication to the community with the Community Awareness and Contribution Award. She is a recipient of the Distinguished Service Medal for Paramedics, recognizing her achievements and contributions to paramedicine. Shannon has been published in the Canadian Paramedicine publication. Shannon holds a Bachelor of Science, Physician Assistant Degree from the University of Toronto School of Community Medicine.

"Death is an inescapable part of life. We can't prevent it; nor can we prevent the inevitable pain of separation it causes. However, we can make the experience of death better, both for the living and the dying."

David Kessler, *The Needs of the Dying*

INTRODUCTION

Death is a complex subject.

It is a time of deep loss, yet it is also a time of reflection and introspection, appreciation, and the opportunity to share intimately with others. For those present for the passing of some, whether as a professional caregiver or as a friend or a family member, it is often viewed as a sacred honor to provide care and comfort at the end of life. Those involved in providing end-of-life care offer education and guidance and compassionate care and support for emotional, spiritual, mental, and practical life wellness and wellbeing. Yes, *wellness and wellbeing* even when someone is approaching death.

Providing end-of-life care can be daunting, yet for those who gravitate to this profession, there is something calling one to serve this vocation. It is an assignment that, even for the seasoned end-of-life caregiver, summons bold courage within, calling up a compassionate character that sometimes surprises. Your fears, worries, and concerns as a new end-of-life practitioner might be: *What do I do if I don't know what to do with a client or their family? What could some of the more unusual end-of-life transitions look like? How do I deal with something difficult? What if I can't handle the reality of providing end-of-life care? Am I going to be good enough as an end-of-life practitioner?*

Or, perhaps you have concerns as an informal caregiver. Maybe you are wondering: *How can I support my family or friend when I haven't had any training? How do I navigate the emotional aspects of caregiving? What if I just can't support them the way they need support? Am I the best person to be providing end-of-life care? Do I need to do this all on my own?*

If any of these questions have ever crossed your mind, this book is for you. Many new end-of-life practitioners or informal caregivers have expressed these same questions and felt insecure, become stuck, or even paralyzed after their initial training, or at the beginning of caring for *their person*, not knowing if they could really do this work. I found answers through mentoring and coaching. Now, I can help you too.

You will easily find yourself exploring one chapter after another in this book as each author, carefully selected to share their experiences, brings exceptional value that will give you the confidence and courage to summon your bold spirit. They open their hearts and souls, often exposing very vulnerable glimpses of themselves.

Offered in this book are experiences, so you can draw your own conclusions as you begin to shape your unique approach to end-of-life caregiving. The book was created in this way because I believe in the power of mentoring — learning through shared experience through stories and examples.

The chapters are written by end-of-life practitioners spanning new to more veteran levels of experience. They all apply because we can learn from all of them. The co-authors come from a variety of roles, including nurse, death educator, certified in the field of thanatology; Indigenous counselor, spiritual practitioner, entrepreneur; paramedic, advanced care paramedic; end-of-life planner, educator, business consultant; medical advocate, caregiver, end-of-life doula, cancer survivor; registered nurse, founding partner of a health management company, director of hospice, death doula; death positive coach; personal support worker; certified end-of-life doula and hypnosis specialist, educator, life and business coach, entrepreneur; hospice/palliative care nurse, end-of-life coach, educator.

This is not a solo effort. You don't have to journey through your end-of-life practice or caregiving experience on your own. Whether you are already well on your way or just want to be better prepared for what may lie ahead, this book will prepare you to go to the next level of inner confidence and in your caregiving.

The truth is, most end-of-life practitioners and caregivers haven't experienced everything under the sun. Even the brightest among us had to start somewhere and learn how to navigate providing the best care possible. It frustrates me to see someone not move forward in a career path they are so passionate about or to learn about a caregiver who has stepped away from a loved one because they didn't feel confident enough in their ability. If this describes you, this book will help you connect with the motivation that once got you started on this rewarding journey.

This book offers support and guidance for your journey into end-of-life care whether you are a formal (paid) or informal (unpaid, family or friend or volunteer) caregiver.

In addition to the caregiving stories, the co-authors open up about:

What was taboo – you will gain a better understanding of some taboo areas so you can be better prepared to deal with them when they arise — and they will.

Resources the practitioners tapped into – some of the resources you will already know, and others will be fresh ideas for you to consider for yourself or to suggest to others.

Tips for practitioners – I imagine you want to quickly excel as an end-of-life practitioner and care provider so this section in the chapters is sure to be beneficial to you.

The impact of the experience on the practitioner – there is always something we can learn from what we encounter, resist, surrender to, or endure. These reflections offer valuable insights.

Moments of revelation – this is like finding a wellspring, allowing you to explore what revelations you have experienced already.

What the end-of-life practitioner wish they had known when they started – with this, you can consider for yourself if you want to examine the topic more thoroughly through online courses, books, additional training, or (my favorite) mentoring.

It is a toss-up to say what the actual highlight of the book will be for you, as every reader comes to this book with a unique perspective and with needs that are different yet common in so many ways. Seriously. I thought the above-noted sections were the highlight, and yet, you will read thoughts on what comprises a **bold spirit** for each of those involved in the end-of-life experience. Plus, you will read what makes these end-of-life practitioners bold spirits. These may surprise you.

If that weren't enough, each caregiving story references "the needs of the dying," developed by David Kessler, death and grieving expert. This component was essential to me when originally defining the parameters of the book because, as David Kessler writes as the subtitle to his acclaimed book, *The Needs of the Dying*, the sixteen needs are "A Guide for Bringing Hope, Comfort, and Love to Life's Final Chapter." I see them as a foundation on which to build an oath or promise of duty as a caregiver to someone in their final days. You will find the actual list at the end of the book.

And finally, I hope you enjoy this book. Take what works and leave the rest but I warn you, there won't be much to leave. If you're ready to explore our collective world of end-of-life caregiving experience, then please read on.

CHAPTER 1

DEATH LESSONS FOR LIFE

"Our new developed and healthy respect for dying and death will strengthen us on both the personal and societal levels."

~ Kortes-Miller, 2018

You need to be aware that conversations about dying, loss, and grief are not always easy. Sometimes, in these conversations, things may come up for you—memories or things you may not have thought about, tender memories of your own experience with death, dying, and loss. I encourage you to take good care of yourself. If you need to stop reading, stop, take some time, reflect, journal, cry, talk to a friend. Even those who provide support for those at the end of life need to pay attention to their emotional, physical, and psychosocial responses to their experience. It is often helpful to practice some form of self-care and self-reflection.

As you read, know that I hold a space for you. We often forget ourselves because we are caring for others. It is important that you learn how to care for yourself first. Do what feels right for you. Do the things that you know how to do to care for yourself. One very simple act that everyone can do to "take care" of self is to practice a simple form of mindfulness, such as deep breathing with some form of visualization, to ground oneself into their own body and settle the chatty mind. I utilize visualization for self-care and for accessing my unconscious desires, fears, and concerns. It's a way for me to see different viewing points and perspectives. What I would like to do now is to take a few moments to guide you through a visualization, using it this time as a way to see into the future, into your future at the end of your life.

Visualization Exercise
Please skip if you do not feel comfortable to do at this time.

For a brief moment, I want you to take a few deep breaths. Come into the present moment here and now. Just be present and pay attention to your body. How do you feel? Let go of the hustle and bustle of the day.

Take a few deep breaths. For a few moments, imagine your own dying and death. What might that look like for you? Who might be there? Where do you find yourself? What do you see? What do you smell? What do you feel around you? Just get a sense of your dying and your death.

What is the feeling? What does your body feel like at this moment? Take a moment to reflect.

Now I want you to grab everything you have imagined and feel it one last time and return to the present reality.

It is not always easy to imagine our own dying and death as it often brings up uncomfortable feelings. Take some time to reflect on your experience.

Did you find yourself in a hospital room? Did you find yourself at home? Did you find yourself outside in nature? Where their people around? Were you alone?

Take a few moments to refresh and restore, journal about your insights, take some time to get grounded. Do something creative.

Drink some water. Breathe.

Visualization can often take us to deep levels of our subconscious and unconscious minds, and breathing assists us to ground and connect us to our bodies.

Each of us may have different reflections, inner imaginings of what our end will be, and what we hope it will be for us and those around us. And you may find yourself at the time of your own dying and death at home or in the hospital, out in nature, alone or not. Each of us will die in our own way.

While there are some common truths about dying, death, loss, and grief, how each of us moves through this process is very individual and unique. Our own preparation and planning are often based on who we are as a person, the history we have with dying and death, and the kinds of relationships we have in our life. We really don't know what the end will look like for any of us.

It is not a question of if we will die but when. For those with a terminal illness or an ailment that may shorten their life, the planning and preparing for end-of-life may be a bit easier. They may have more information and knowledge about what they may experience as they are dying and what kind of death they might encounter based on the physical state of their body and the impact of their particular illness. Death will happen to all of us, and I fear that we are ill-prepared for our own dying experience and death.

Someone once asked me when my journey as a "death educator" began. It was a good question, one that I had contemplated before but had never been asked until then. Instead of answering back right away, I allowed the question to sink into my core and held its contemplative embrace. "I think I was in my twenties when I became conscious of the fact that I had a comfort level with all things death-related, but unconsciously it may have started with my family experience," I replied.

My family had a secret that was held very tightly for over twenty-five years. You see, my older brother died only three days after being born. My mother was only twenty years old at the time. It was 1964, Czechoslovakia, and like most approaches to infant loss at the time, my mother was told that she was young and should have another child as soon as possible. The topic was avoided to reduce my parents' suffering, to help them deal with the tragedy. One year and a day, my other brother was born. And I was born five years later, an "unplanned pregnancy." I carried a story for most of my life that my mother had a miscarriage, that she had a "failed" pregnancy, and there was never any mention of my other older brother until I was in my twenties. It was then that my mom shared her story of loss with me. She cried, I cried.

There are so many stories of loss and grief that get stored away, never to be revealed, sometimes even to those closest to the griever. I can only imagine how my parents felt as I do not have any children of my own. Over the last twenty-five years through my professional training, I have learned that grief is very individual and that child loss is one of the hardest losses to integrate and endure. And that kind of loss is even more challenging when that loss is not acknowledged and supported by the griever's family, friends, community, and social systems of society.

Maybe because of this family loss, I began to study human emotions, behavior, and how people navigate through loss. I started my journey into death care as a nurse. I started my training discovering the wonders of the body and its physiology. I studied diverse diseases, chronic illnesses, the dying process, and death. But the fundamental nursing skills did not provide me with enough knowledge to fully support families who were managing and coping with end-of-life challenges and stress. As a young nurse, I still felt ill-equipped to care for those at the end of life, so I continued to seek more information and knowledge about death, dying, loss, and grief.

I think for many of us, death has an impact even when the stories are not told. Without my own awareness, the death of Alexander, my brother, my mother's firstborn, had a big impact on my life.

As a nurse, I was tasked with taking care of residents in long-term care homes who were dying. While I had the training to care for their physical well-being and manage their physical pain and symptoms, nothing really prepared me for being with them during their very uncertain, unknown, and intimate experience, their final hours, their personal dying, and death. I had minimal exposure to dying and death, even as a nurse. And for the many families that I worked with, this was often their first experience with dying and death. And so we supported each other through the experience. I offered what I could to ease their pain. I encouraged them to care for their parents or family member and explained the dying process as best I could based on what I knew at the time. I supported them, and they supported me by inviting me into their family experience and allowing me to learn and grow.

I knew that I needed more knowledge and more experience, so I ventured to gain more training. I took a number of different courses, gained a few certificates and degrees. I have studied and worked in the field of spiritual care, hospice palliative care, adult education, chronic disease management, thanatology, and bereavement. I am a lifelong learner. There is always so much more we can learn. I believe that death education, death literacy, how we care for those who are dying, the dead, and the bereaved shift and transforms through social constructs and time. Dying is not an illness. Dying is like birthing. And the way through labor and delivery is governed by social, environmental, political norms and rules and laws of society to ensure safety, dignity, and respect. But dying and death are also governed by natural laws.

From my learning, I realized that life has a cyclical pattern and that without death, life would not be possible. It may be a bit far-fetched, but I believe that without dying and death and grief, humanity's progression in evolution would not have occurred. Death is needed for us to recognize the preciousness of life and well-being. Dying can teach us to have more compassion and care for self, life, and others.

What I will share with you comes from the many books I have read, the training that I have done, and from my own experiences sitting with the dying and those grieving. Some of what I will share may validate what you already know. Some may contradict what you know, and some will challenge what you may assume to know. It is often the things that we don't know that can be harmful. Education is important and key to so much of our ignorance and fears around dying, death, and grief.

I believe that we are at a time in history where people are searching for better ways of preparing for and planning for the end of life. I have been part of gathering together with those interested in some aspect of end-of-life care and how to shift the way we approach its process for those we care about, including ourselves.

Historically dying and death care was held in the hands of the family and community members, laywomen and men, who served to care for the dying and dead. In many traditional or orthodox faith communities, this still happens today. The process of planning, preparing, caring for the dying and the dead are still done by those who are not considered "professionals" but by those tasked by their community to support such end-of-life care. The way of our "modern" deathcare has been influenced by individual, collective, social, cultural, political, and economic views, shifts, and interests.

I have been at the bedside of those dying, and I've asked them some of the following questions. "What is it that people really need to know before they go? What would you share?" And they often say very simple things. "I wish I could have spent more time with my kids; it would have been great to have my whole family here." "I have some regrets about the things that I've done." "Can you help me to die well?"

Many have said, "If I knew then what I know now, I probably would have done things a little differently." I hold the experiences that I have had with the dying persons and all of their families as moments of death awareness. They are, for me, death lessons for life. I can still hear their voices telling me, "I wish I had more time with my family"; "I wish I would have done the thing that I love to do"; "I wish I took more risks"; and "I wish I would have spoken from the heart, but I was too afraid." This is how death has taught me to live a full life, be present with all of it, and make peace with dying and death.

Our views are changing. We have a desire for death education—death awareness. We have a yearning for conversations that have been hidden. We have forgotten that death is present within all living things.

Women are often a little bit closer to the natural death cycles. Women's menstrual blood can be seen as small deaths of those unplanted pregnancies. In nature, winter is the dying time with change—death cycles. The way of dying and birthing is natural and vital to life.

So how can you prepare for the inevitable?

Step One: You are already doing it. You have the willingness to read about, hear about and have conversations about death and dying. I believe that it is our human right and a need to understand the process of dying and death so that we may be better prepared for the unknown. Education is often the key to reduce fears, concerns, and worries. And sharing our stories of dying, death, and grief helps all of us to feel less alone and helpless, knowing there are others who share a similar experience.

Step Two: You might want to start journaling or taking notes of your values that are important to you, those that you want to sustain and maintain as you're reaching your dying and death. What will it look like, who will be there? Part of our own adult responsibility is to participate in decisions concerning our own care and to have our questions answered honestly and fully. From my experience, emotions within families who often have to make hard decisions at the end of life are more challenging when "wishes and wants" are not addressed or talked about. Like Dr. Kortes-Miller said, "Talking about death won't kill you," and it may make the journey at the end a bit better.

Step Three: Gain the information and learn about advance care planning, the process for choosing and talking with those that would have the power and authority to make decisions on your behalf if you were not able, for future health care, including at the time of your dying and death. Learning about the laws that govern health care consent and end-of-life and post-death care are important to know so that those who will care for you during the labors of dying and post-death ensure your dignity, your wishes, your values.

Step Four: And finally, continue to be curious. If you have an opportunity to do some volunteer work, sit at the bedside. Welcome the invitation and give thanks for the opportunity to be with others and see that everyone's death and dying and grief are very individual based on who they are, their history, their relationship, where they come from, and the worldview they hold.

Death, dying, and grief place us in the space of the unknown and often chaotic change in our everyday reality. Often it shatters that which grounds us in safety, stability, and security.

There can be pain with dying, not only because of illness, pains of the physical body but also from emotional pain, psychosocial and spiritual pain. Someone who has lived a long life may have pain because of the regrets that they may feel. Most of the time, people who are dying need someone to listen, to hear their story, someone to bear witness to their end of life, to hear the totality of who they were in the good and the bad, in the beautiful and the horrible.

I believe that before we die, we all want to tell our life story one last time, to immortalize ourselves somehow, to ensure that we are remembered somehow. Some death philosophers such as Stephen Jenkinson (Jenkinson, 2015) suggest that the reason why we, in the Western world, are in "death denial" and why we may find ourselves struggling in life is that we haven't sustained and maintained the relationships to those who have come before us. He suggests that we have lost our connection to our ancestors.

It takes courage to go back and have those conversations with the people who have died, whether they be your grandparents, parents, brother, sister, aunt, uncle, or children. Having these conversations is part of integrating the loss through mourning, a social way to grief which validates and normalizes our process. Some of us may have some unfinished business with the person who has died. We can call out the person and talk to them about the things we were thankful for, the things we were really angry about. And the ways in which they may have hurt us and what they meant to us in life.

I strive to have good relationships with those in my immediate and intimate circle. I hope that I will be there when my parents die, but I know that I cannot make promises. Life's situations and experiences can often be unpredictable, and sometimes things happen that you may not have expected. I do my best not to make promises, to understand that extraordinary things may happen. The year 2020 will be remembered for being unpredictable and extraordinary. I hope that I am able to support my parents at their end of life because that is meaningful for me. And I will strive to remember my connection to them after they die.

What I have seen over the years and what the research suggests is that when a person is dying, they have another level of awareness and can communicate with their ancestors. When people are dying and close to death, they sometimes get over-sensitive; they become sensitive to stimulation, which sometimes creates restlessness. And as they spend more time sleeping, sometimes it's hard for the family members because they still want to spend a lot of time with them. Bit by bit, the dying person is detaching from the relationship established in the physical realm and may start to reconnect with those that have already died.

What factors, if any, contribute to an increasing anxiety in relation to death? What happens in a changing field of medicine, where we have to ask ourselves whether medicine is to remain a humanitarian and respected profession or a new but depersonalized science in the service of prolonging life rather than diminishing human suffering. (Kübler-Ross, 1969)

The above words were written more than fifty years ago by Elisabeth Kübler-Ross, who was instrumental in opening the doorway to end-of-life knowledge, research, and continued interest in death literacy. Dr. Kübler-Ross and the small book *On Death and Dying*, published in 1969, influenced so much of my early studies and work in end-of-life care. The real stories of those navigating their end of life enriched so much of my nursing studies as I began to be more aware of the complexities of dying, death, and grief, and provided a personal narrative inclusive of psychosocial and spiritual concerns.

I have had the honor and privilege to provide end-of-life education to those interested in the topic since 2015. I have always felt a level of comfort talking about the things that are often difficult to talk about, such as preparing and planning for dying, death and grief. At the core, I have a bold spirit that is willing to question how we approach dying and death and do my own work to expand my awareness and knowledge before offering to guide others in their journey.

As an end-of-life nurse educator who sees death as a teacher and its ability to change our perception, our outlook on life, I am hopeful that if enough people have conversations about the things that matter to them at the end of life, then maybe we can bring more death awareness into the public sphere and realize that having this dialogue around death and dying can bring more life to our everyday experience. It can bring life to the world or at least to be able to offer every single one of us the right to have as much life as we can before we physically die.

I send compassion and gratitude to those that care for people who are at the end of life.

ಏ ಐ

What was taboo

Talking about death and dying was and remains to be taboo. There is a sense that if you wish to talk about death, it must mean that you wish to die. Often talking about death and preparing for the inevitable enables us to be more present with every moment because there is a deep understanding that one day we will die. I also believe that talking about vulnerable emotions like grief is something that is now becoming less taboo. People want to educate themselves on better ways to be with those that are grieving, not wanting to move them towards acceptance but giving them space to grieve in their own way. Western society is often very fearful of strong emotions like grief, which may be why we often medicate grieving those. In the past, I often felt like no one wanted to speak about the end of life and how to better prepare. I am glad that things are changing, that we are willing to speak the unspeakable.

Resources I tapped into

Over the past twenty-five years, I have read a number of books on death, dying, loss and grief. I have explored the world of thanatology, the study of death and dying, and have developed a real drive to learn more about all aspects of end-of-life care, both within the health care field and education. And while it is good to expand one's knowledge through study and reading, it has really been my personal experience that has enabled me to "tap into" my own resilience and passion for death literacy.

Moment of revelation

I have had a few aha moments over the years as an end-of-life nurse educator. I recognized early on that end-of-life care needs to be wholistic, and person/family-centered and that "it takes a village" to provide wrap-around care and support. In addition, I have recognized that I cannot do this alone, that I must work within an interdisciplinary team-based model. I have also realized that the learnings from being with the dying and the bereaved often arrive when your own life changes and brings you to your own grieving experience. In those moments of personal experience, I rely on the teachings and knowledge that I have obtained throughout my career.

Self-care tips that helped me

A very simple care tip that I always come back to in my professional and personal life is mindful breathing. A simple breathing technique such as box breathing can bring me back to center and ground me in the present moment. I take a breath in and count for four seconds, clearing my mind, hold the breath for four seconds, grounding myself, exhale for a count of four, and let go of any tension and stress, and finally, hold again empty for four seconds. I repeat this cycle until my mind quiets and my body feels at ease. You can do it anywhere, anytime.

Tips for practitioners

Be authentic and true to your own nature. There are many ways that end-of-life practitioners support their clients, and often we are witness to very private and intimate details and life experiences. Providing support takes a team-based approach, a compassionate community that is willing to create a sacred space for dying, death and grief. Because being witness to this very intimate life experience is so unique and personal, we must be authentic and real with the people we work with.

What I wish I had known when I began on this journey as a practitioner in end-of-life care and what I discovered about it

I wish I would have known then what I know now, but I know that is not possible, and maybe that is why I teach. Knowledge is power, and when we are better informed about our life experience, including our end of life, we can make better choices and decisions based on awareness and not fear. I learn to better understand my own life experience and share what I have learned and what I still need to learn in an effort to enhance the care we provide to those facing end of life.

The impact this experience had on me

I continue to be impacted by my experiences, my life choices to educate others about death, dying, and grief. I can now see that my own life has always had weavings of loss. My quest for knowledge about end of life and what that means to our human evolution has allowed me to see the preciousness of our human experience its vulnerability.

A self-care tip for caregivers

The best advice I can give to caregivers is to remember to breathe, remember that the most painful moment is only that moment. Ultimately everything must change. Breathing helps us to gain the energy we need to move forward to engage with all of the experiences with dying, death and grief. And if you can bring more of the elements of nature into your every day, the better your integration will be.

ഔ ൕ

How are end-of-life practitioners bold spirits?

End-of-life practitioners are often willing to speak about the things many people aren't willing to speak about, such as death, dying, loss, and grief.

It can be very challenging for end-of-life practitioners to hold space for another. It requires much self-reflection and honesty in their skills and abilities. In addition, many struggle with being good enough, acknowledging that there is an innate ability of all of us to be present at someone's end of life, but it requires a lot of courage.

The end-of-life practitioner doesn't have the answers. So their bold spirit is also saying, "I am willing to sit with you. I'm willing to be with you. And I have no idea what this is going to be like for you." Most end-of-life practitioners have spent time studying and training in the field of thanatology, hospice, palliative, or end-of-life care. They have often experienced loss and have been present with those that have died. Some are called to study and train for this work in an effort to do things better, to do death differently, to bring more joy, beauty, and compassion to end-of-life care.

Bold spirits include people like Kathy Kortes-Miller, Rami Shami, and Dr. Naheed Dosani. They often do things that are sometimes seen as outside of the status quo, attempting to shift how we view end-of-life and how we deliver end-of-life care to all people that promote self-determination and dignity. I think end-of-life practitioners are willing to adapt and learn and push the edges sometimes. They're willing to educate, advocate, and empower everyone around end-of-life care.

How is the informal caregiver (non-paid family or friend) a bold spirit?

When we're present with somebody else's death, we are confronted with our own mortality. This is especially true for caregivers because their world as they know it is ending. Their relationship with their person is coming to an end. When they are able to have the courage to stay with that, that's bold. Sometimes I think we as a society make a demand saying, "Well, you're the caregiver; it's what you're supposed to do." But caregivers may not always have the skills or the coping mechanisms or the resources to "be" with their person at the end of life and require education, guidance, and support.

Our current health care system isn't always conducive to what people need. On the one hand, the message caregivers are given is "Call me any time," but on the other hand, "but only call me between 8:30 and 4:30." It doesn't make sense. And while much of the focus is on the dying person and their experience to alleviate as much of the suffering to make them comfortable, caregivers have needs too because they are trying to cope with what's happening while their whole world, as they know it, comes to an end.

This is part of what I believe we don't think enough about, and perhaps as a society, we're coming to understand better. The impact of loss is significant, not only the death of a person but also the losses of hopes and dreams, loss of the relationship, along primary and secondary losses.

The caregiver is the one who is sustaining the care at the end of life. The end-of-life practitioner is there too but may only be there for an hour or two or giving the caregiver some insight or resources, but the caregiver has to sustain that level of being in the space that is so, so hard to do.

The practitioner can leave it. The practitioner can say, "It's not working for me; I'm leaving it." But the caregiver can't necessarily leave, although many people do—think of the adult children or siblings that don't stick around through the caregiving. And so again, we need to expand our understanding of the informal caregiver, their challenges, and how we can best support them. We may also underestimate that caregivers care out of duty or because there are no other choices or options for care. How do we acknowledge the boldness and the resiliency of those who stay even though it's not out of a heart space but out of duty or obligation or guilt?

How is the dying person a bold spirit?

The individual dying is the one going into the unknown before we do. There's a question new death doulas often get tripped up on when asked in training. The question is: "How does the person dying still contribute to society?" People don't necessarily acknowledge that when a person is dying, they often enable us to see human vulnerability. The dying person offers us the gift of learning how to be present with dying, death, and loss and do it a bit differently. That's why *Tuesdays with Morrie* by Mitch Albom was so popular. It allowed those who have not been present with dying to get a sense of what the dying person goes through when approaching their end of life.

What makes you a bold spirit in terms of end-of-life practitioner work?

There's something in my DNA because this isn't something that I discovered in my later years. I think my interest in death, dying, loss, and grief has always been there. I recently said to someone, "You can't take the end-of-life out Olga." This is part of it. I've always been big on transformation and death to the old and birth to the new. I'm always willing to learn. So I can't separate that out of me. I have been known to be a change agent, an agitator, a trickster, to be the person who asks many questions and offers a different viewing point. The reflection back from others has often been, "That's a really interesting thought. I never thought of it that way." "That's an interesting reflection."

I think death and transformation are an ongoing part of my life. Sometimes it's tough when everything is changing—dying. Everything, including some of my own concepts, ideas about what I thought, what I thought this life would be like, has been transformed. But I continue to do the work even though it's hard, even though it puts me in loss, even though it breaks my world apart sometimes. But I come back to it. I come back to the teachings of the spiritual guides of that transformative process. It's hard to separate it. I think I have something in my DNA, and maybe it stems from a past life, I don't know. I think my life story speaks to this transformative element a little bit. In one of the shamanic practices, one of the techniques is to write your story, the story of your most wounded self, the darkest of the dark one last time so that you can leave it behind. There is power in writing your own story one last time, letting go of the past, and letting the past die, including the old self. Writing your life story one last time allows you to reclaim some of the power that you lost. And this requires deep changes inside of us.

To me, death and death education, death awareness, end-of-life, transitions, or life process is so much more than being present with someone who's dying. It's an everyday part of our life that reminds us that life continues to change. I know I'm not the same person I was last year or the year before or even last week because of all of the things that have happened. I know that, and I'm okay with that. I want to be better. I want to grow. I want to let go of the old patterns that no longer serve me. I continue to let go of negative patterns.

As an end-of-life practitioner, I want . . .

. . . to be able to channel my gifts in the most appropriate way.

I want to channel my gifts to have a positive impact in the world and on those that I work with and serve. While the pandemic has restricted so much of our communication and connection, it has provided greater opportunities for those that want to learn about end-of-life care. Technology enables us to connect across the world, gather together, share, and learn together. Fundamentally I am an educator, and I love to share my knowledge and skills with those that wish to learn. I am adding my boldness to the death awareness movement.

ಶ್ರೀ ಛಿ

Olga Nikolajev, RN, MA, CT, CE

Olga is an End-of-Life Nurse Educator certified in the field of thanatology. Olga has a Master's degree in Religion and Culture, several multidisciplinary certificates, including a certificate in cannabis science from McMaster University. Olga facilitates Thanatology and End-of-Life Doula courses across Canada and provides support as a Grief Counselor to formal and informal caregivers. She has provided educational presentations and facilitated many workshops over the last ten years in death and grief literacy. In addition, Olga is guiding the work of the Death Doula Ontario Network, which she founded in 2020.

Contact information:

www.dyingmatters.ca
613-921-2231
olganikolajev@xplornet.ca

Book Recommended by Olga Nikolajev

Final Gifts: Understanding the Special Awareness, Needs, and Communications of the Dying
by Maggie Callanan and Patricia Kelley (2012)

The collection of narratives and experiences in this book reveals that dying has a spiritual and sometimes mystical element and that we, as those who care, can learn to better understand the "secret language" in an effort to continue to communicate and provide comfort at the end of life.

About the Book

"In this moving and compassionate classic—now updated with new material from the authors—hospice nurses Maggie Callanan and Patricia Kelley share their intimate experiences with patients at the end of life, drawn from more than twenty years' experience tending the terminally ill.

Through their stories we come to appreciate the near-miraculous ways in which the dying communicate their needs, reveal their feelings, and even choreograph their own final moments; we also discover the gifts—of wisdom, faith, and love—that the dying leave for the living to share.

Filled with practical advice on responding to the requests of the dying and helping them prepare emotionally and spiritually for death, Final Gifts shows how we can help the dying person live fully to the very end." ~ Amazon

CHAPTER 2

GROUNDED IN CULTURE

"We are related to everything above us and below us."

~ gkisedtanamoogk, Knowledge Keeper

It had been a long journey, but finally, setting my feet on the frozen ground made me turn my gaze towards the mountains. Their strength and fortitude arm the landscape in my old home of Thunder Bay. It was April in northern Ontario, and spring had decided it wasn't going to come.

My grandma had just turned fifty-eight, and I didn't know at the time how young that still was. I myself had been nineteen for a few months, but my three-month-old son had aged me considerably. It would be years until I realized how little I knew about the world, but they say that is the curse of youth, wasted on the young.

She had been a constant in my life, a force to be reckoned with that both of my parents seemed to magically fear and abide by. When I had sat down a few years before and heard about her big C breast cancer, I wasn't worried for even a moment.

"She'll beat that. Grandma is tougher than cancer." A small half-smile crept onto my grandpa's face, and he looked at his wife. They had been together since they were fourteen, and forty-four years later, this tiny, five-foot woman was the whole of his universe. Over the next two years, she would lose the curls that formed her famous helmet of hair, rock all of the turbans, and boldly wear her baby brush cut with pride once she'd gotten the news from the doctor that she was in remission.

"I told you," I said with smugness. Our family had always been spread apart, reunited by twenty-hour car rides and the promises of bonfires and swimming brought by warm weather. Most holidays, we were apart, and this felt normal to me as I went about my life, getting into trouble with an abusive relationship, the law, and then even more with a baby on the way.

She never faltered standing in front of the judge who held zero doubts about her abilities to reform me, bailing me out of jail, then swooping me back up north, safe in her circle of protection.

When cancer returned, this time it was with a vengeance, and there would be no remission or recovery. I refused to falter in my faith in her. She would beat this too. *It's who she is*, I thought to myself.

When the call from my mother came, I was utterly unprepared. "She's not going to last long. I'm booking your plane tickets. You need to come now." I had never been on a plane, but it wasn't the time to marvel at new experiences. My grandmother was dying. Arriving the next afternoon, we were picked up at the airport and went straight to the hospital.

She was a woman who would have been known today as a homesteader—canning food, knitting clothes, and stitching bedding, artfully crafting the entirety of the family's holiday decor. For the first time in my life, this woman whom I had towered over since age ten looked frail and weak.

She could barely breathe but wanted to hold her first great-grandchild. She had bought him knitted socks from the gift shop, knowing she would never make him anything herself. This was the first real dagger of loss I felt, breaking through the numbness of seeing my grandma that way.

She quickly grew too tired and dozed off. My grandpa said we should come back tomorrow, and that night, she let go.

The next afternoon we were gathered at the funeral parlor, around her made-up body in a tasteful coffin. We were a small family of six in that room—my grandpa, uncle, aunt, mother, myself, and my son crowded around her in the only viewing that would take place. The cigarettes placed with her in the coffin upset me, and I did what my grandma taught me to do—I spoke up.

I was outraged that cigarettes had taken my grandmother from me and couldn't see past it; those cigarettes symbolized her murder. After all, how else could such a powerful matriarch be felled? My mother, aunt, and uncle tried to reason with me, though without success. To this day, I remain one of the more stubborn in our family tree. A stern word from my grandpa silenced us all, but I carried the anger like another baby, and it disconnected me from her grief in a way that I couldn't comprehend at the time.

Later I would understand that my family couldn't offer me this teaching because, to a degree, they didn't have it to offer. Only time and lived experience with cultural reclamation would ease my grief from the place of anger where I had it deeply lodged, within.

You see, our family carries lived experience as intergenerational Indian Residential School survivors on my grandfather's side, and my grandmother herself was a Métis woman. What my family could not teach me that day was that tobacco is one of the sacred medicines used to honor and connect with our ancestors during times of ceremony and prayer.

Like the coins on the eyes of the deceased, tobacco would ensure that my grandma's spirit journeyed safely back to the Sky World.

My grandmother has been gone for over twenty years now, and as an Indigenous death worker, the ways that I seek out traditional death practices can be clearly traced back to a time and a place when I struggled with all I didn't know. So much has been lost from our ancestors' ways of living, practices once passed from generation to generation. I strive to create space where we can honor what has survived by taking steps forward in a contemporary and healing way.

I would choose to honor my grandma, who believed in reincarnation when my daughter was born, six years later, by giving her my grandma's nickname to walk with in this life. Later, when I became an undergraduate, I was determined to learn more and would go on to reclaim all that I could, in her honor, and to ensure my children didn't struggle with who they were or where they belonged. I found comfort in lean times and sickness by praying to my grandma, who was now my ancestor, looking out for my children and me like I knew she would have in life. My mind swelled with memories at the sight of the cardinal when it visited, her most favorite bird, which often appeared when gathered with my uncle or cousins.

As an Anishinaabekwe and member of the Pikwakanagan First Nation, I am proud to say that I have begun walking a path that slowly brings me closer and closer to my purpose as an Omamiwininiiwiikwe or Algonquin woman. As an Indigenous death worker, there is a knowing of harm reduction and its role in every aspect of support. This knowing is sometimes called blood memory; other times, it is referred to as intuition. No matter the term, Indigenous death workers are increasingly being called on to offer care for those facing death, dying, loss and grief.

Harm reduction for First Nations, Inuit, and Métis people living in rural, suburban and urban spaces look like advocating for the right to a good death. Some of us began as birth and reproductive health doulas, and this work took shape in places of pregnancy loss and infertility. Others found a path from grief over the loss of missing and murdered Indigenous family members and loved ones to prevent the genocide by a systemic force of racism that has worked diligently for hundreds of years to exterminate our families at every given opportunity. Today, as I write, I am reminded of the environmental racism that plagues our communities and tasks Indigenous land and water defenders with the work of risking their own lives to fight for our survival as a species, even while a pandemic ravages the globe.

The idea to launch a grassroots Indigenous Death Doula Collective came about naturally in response to a gap in knowledge and culturally-grounded training opportunities. Since its formation, the Blackbird Medicines' Indigenous Death Doula Collective has undertaken several projects and continues to serve our respective communities in new and expanding ways.

Modern Canadian society continues to demonstrate for First Nations, Inuit, and Métis families that they are unsafe in public institutions and their rights, the rights of their loved ones are not upheld or respected. It is arguable that Indigenous peoples are consistently working to reduce impacts and harms that would result in early death, some from the moment of birth. A child removed from its mother is fighting to survive that separation, and the mother whose child is removed must fight her own notions and internalized feelings of racism and inadequacies. With one separation, there are two fights taking place against death and failure to thrive.

While Blackbird Medicines is a healing practice offering community care, it was important to launch the collective grassroots effort for Indigenous death workers, and like so much of this journey, once it was offered up, the demand caught on like wildfire. After several years in frontline social service work, I had grown frustrated with program restrictions that seemed to leave folks outside of circles of care. The Indigenous Death Doula Collective highlighted that other Indigenous care providers felt similar, and the collective need of NDN country to reclaim caregiver teachings continues to resound loudly as I attempt to walk a path I never anticipated being on.

As Indigenous death doulas, we recognize the fight to survive and the right to die of old age, in safety, in security, housed, surrounded by loved ones, and free of pain. As Indigenous death doulas, we address and support those dying as they face a lack of family connection due to historical oppression, often undertaking genealogical work and cultural education that fosters a sense of community and pride.

Endayan Mashkiki means my home medicine in Anishinaabemowin and is the name of our medicine bundle project to provide traditional medicines and wellness practices to our communities to better cope with the difficulties of isolation, poverty, loss, and grief created by the pandemic lockdowns.

Gathering my home medicines was the inspiration of my own journey; to reclaim what I would have learned had colonization not interfered with my family. What might have happened if my grandfather had maintained his childhood fluency in Anishinaabemowin? What if his own mother hadn't felt her safest option was to raise demonstrably committed Catholics, to prevent her children from being apprehended like her husband? Like herself?

Through attempts to bridge gaps in knowledge around death and dying by offering support, insights, and pathways to reclaiming culture and an understanding of a good death, I found a way to keep my grandma's spirit alive within me. The oldest daughter in a family of eighteen, my grandma carried teachings as a caregiver and passed on far more to me than I realized before she left.

Indigenous families who are faced with the death of a loved one or their own end-of-life plans are forced to factor in financial costs, travel, risks to personal safety and that of extended family, as well as respect of the deceased, legislation, and the commercialization of final arrangements. This work to reclaim an understanding has led me to Ontario legislation and rights of the dying and how that intersects with Indigenous rights, federally, on and off reserve, for status and non-status Indigenous people.

Through private death cafes and family counseling, the Indigenous Death Doula Collective has empowered families to discuss death and normalize that aspect of life, reducing stress, trauma, and fear of the unknown. This has been particularly powerful in the midst of a pandemic and horrific displays of systemic racism.

The importance of inter-generational care and knowledge transmission by doing are exactly the spirit of caregiver teachings that my grandma gifted me. Caregiver teachings are one way that we can empower the reclamation of culture. Our collective will continue to role model how one can take pride in their role as protectors and teachers, just like my grandma taught me. Caregiver teachings are one way that we can empower the reclamation of culture. Our collective continues to demonstrate for parents and guardians how one can reclaim and take pride in their role as protectors and teachers.

Many Indigenous people struggle with the intergenerational impacts of colonization. For Black, Indigenous, People of Color (BIPOC) from other territories who find themselves living on this continent we call Turtle Island, there are older stories of colonization and genocide carried in their DNA that most of us know little about. These stories of resistance and survival have a place too, and the right to die a good death is something not afforded to many of us, our families, or the generations before, and this, we carry too.

As a bold spirit, I will continue to honor my caregiver teachings by sharing space with those who need to tell their own stories, by using my white privilege to amplify the voices of others, and continuously work to decenter whiteness.

୫ଠ ଔ

What was taboo

It was taboo to try and work with my community when no one knew who I was. It was also the key to unlock the door, leading to a path that led to my community. They say nothing easy is worth doing!

Resources I tapped into

The resource I tapped into which was beneficial to me on this learning journey was Barb Phillips, a Thanadoula. By taking Barb's "Home Funeral How-To" training, I connected with other practitioners in my area while also learning about legislation and best practices for this work as an end-of-life caregiver. Signing up for Barb's course was a catalyst for me, and I am grateful for her accessible, community-style of bringing others into this work.

Moment of revelation

There have been several moments of revelation on this journey, and what stands out most right now is the reckoning I faced when writing my chapter. I didn't realize I had the insights that I did into my grandmother's death until it flowed from my fingers, with tears streaming down my face. Sometimes, a moment to sit with your thoughts can have more impact than we know. Sometimes we need to reflect and take inventory on what we do know!

Self-care tips that helped me

There is no special trick, though I do benefit from a practice of grounding myself, which I began in my early thirties. As a survivor of trauma and a chronic pain warrior, mental dissociation is an ongoing reality from my physical self, and this is particularly relevant when I am struggling with feeling overwhelmed, experiencing high levels of stress, or a pain flare. Learning to slow down and remain still in a moment is a tonic. I can tap into this stillness through ceremony, practice of my culture, and use traditional medicines, yoga, meditation, and time on the land. Puppies are also helpful, and for this reason, I have three.

The truth is that I am not great at self-care. It does not come naturally. The opposite comes naturally to me, and I have experienced burnout several times in my life and career. Writing has always been my catharsis, a gentle hug to my psyche, and so this book has been its own medicine. Miigwetch

Tip or strategy to help other caregivers

Sometimes we don't know what we don't know, and that is okay. Unlearning can be filled with pain, memories, and feelings of discomfort. The only thing to do is to lean in and embrace the awkward. It does get easier.

Tips for practitioners

Practitioners of end-of-life care must face their own passion and interest, no matter where it comes from, and put their energy to use. There are endless ways to approach this calling and one is only limited by their own imagination and preferences.

Time and again, this work on the frontlines can grow difficult and weigh my spirit with a heaviness. Pay attention to this and answer the calling to slow your pace. The greatest skill a caregiver can develop is the ability to set boundaries and develop a practice of care for the self. We must rest, reflect, and offer care to ourselves, just as we would help others do on this path.

The impact on me from this experience

This experience was unique and important for my own development as a caregiver and community leader. To take pause and reflect on the journey here has been important and healing. I did not realize how closely I carried my grandmother's death in my younger years, until the revelation was before me on the screen. I am going to carry this experience with me for a long time and am excited to have played a role.

What I wish I had known when I began on this journey as a practitioner in end-of-life care and what I discovered about it

I wish I had known at the beginning how in-demand my practice as an Indigenous death worker and end-of-life care practitioner would be. My own journey left me struggling to fill gaps of knowledge as someone raised without connections to culture or identity. Embarking on this journey as an Indigenous death worker has connected me to many others who crave the same reclamation of caregiver teachings, and that is a gift of community care.

ဢ ൟ

How are end-of-life practitioners bold spirits?

When I think about the people that I'm surrounded by and the people I try and engage to take on this work, the bold spirits are really just trying to build bridges and connect people at their end of life. And we know that connection is the cure to aches, to so much emotional turmoil. Connection is always that solution. So when I think about who those bold spirits are, it's those folks that are rallying for that connection. And it's not always the people who find connection to be easy, especially with Indigenous communities. So many folks have, and I'm no exception at all, challenging role models or learned behaviors around connection, or there's trauma there that has fractured their understanding of connection. A lot of times, not only are you trying to support people in end-of-life care, but you're also embarking on a really tough journey of unlearning.

If unlearning doesn't make you a bold spirit, to sit in your discomfort and embrace it and what you don't know, I mean, what the heck does?

How are caregivers bold spirits?

Think of those moments when they want to break down, but they don't because they know that they're holding everyone else up. It's those folks that, maybe it's the brother-in-law, maybe it's not someone that's born into the family, still showing up and contributing to that family connection just the same. With family members, it can be so complicated because we all have these different roles. There are different perceptions for the youngest, the middle, the mother, the "whomever," and there's so much that goes with that. But when we think about those family members, those unsung heroes that are there in that connection space, it's easy enough to turn away. It's easy enough not to be the sibling helping, and it's easy to be the family member who lives too far away. It's easy to think that someone else will step up to care for a loved one as they are preparing to die. It takes bravery to show up, to stay, and navigate unknown waters. To show up and to say, "I don't know what I'm doing, but I'm here to help. I don't think I can do anything, but I'm here" makes for bold spirits in these people who are standing up when they're called on.

Being a caregiver is not for the faint of heart. And honestly, it's not recognized work most of the time. Our society repeatedly devalues caregivers. And even now, in this pandemic, we hear again and again and again that our caregivers aren't being taken care of.

And so it's that bold spirit that really makes me think of them going to do what they think is right no matter what, whether they're paid or not. But to be that bold spirit and to occupy that role as a caregiver, without thanks, without payment, you're not only supporting that person at the end of their life, you're role modeling it to the other members of your family of this is what caregiving looks like. It's thankless work, and it's always the same people that do it.

There's this inner calling to just take care of others. And again, with the indigenous community perspective, a lot of those people do double whammies, and they end up in social work, and they're the caregivers in their family. They're taking on children that they didn't birth. There are many people who are committed to supporting, as that bold spirit, without payment, without recognition. And how radical to think that this is a book that's coming out for those people. That's something that's really, really moved me in this whole project. This is for them.

How is the person dying a bold spirit?

At the end of life, there's so much there. Whether you are a young person who has received an unexpected shortening to your lifespan, or you're that ninety-some-year-old grandma that's seen a lot and lived a lot and enjoys life, surrounded by great-grandchildren and grandchildren, there's never an easy way. Sometimes I talk to people about end-of-life and embracing what's ahead of them. The person who's facing the wick as it's running out, there's so much that they're confronted with, whether it's stories that they wish had been played out differently, stories they crafted to ease their memories, stories they tell that are memories, it's a lot. We are basically the sum of our stories.

At that end of life, I just can't think of a more bold task to face those life stories. But also, there can be real frustration and anguish when we look at those stories of what we didn't accomplish or what we didn't convey at that time that we should have. Those regret pieces can be daunting, and those bold spirits are facing that, but they're also often facing the pain of their loved ones and saying goodbye. There is also fear. Lots of times, there's so much fear about what their families are going to be left with after they're gone.

Just because the dying person doesn't have their kids at home or their mother next to them, it doesn't mean that they're going to stop thinking about them and worrying about them. And right to the last minute, they might be worrying, "Oh my goodness. I don't know if my daughter is going to be able to stay housed," and concerning themselves with how others will fare once they have died. It can be a battle that they have to face.

I am reminded of the Serenity Prayer: "the power to change what I can and the wisdom to know the difference." Dying is not for the faint of heart. At some point, if it's possible, and a person can find some peace with what's going to happen or some semblance of acceptance, that is certainly an element of being a bold spirit. It's hard enough to live and live well, but to die and die well, sometimes there's just so little in our control.

What makes you a bold spirit as an end-of-life practitioner?

My own life. My own loves. My own family. My own connections. That's what drives me. I'm a parent, and being a parent has compelled me to do more things in my whole life than I never thought I would ever do. I was one of these young people that didn't really know what I wanted to do, right up until probably my mid- or late twenties. I was clueless. I knew I was good at things, but I didn't know how to channel that or what would make me happy channeling that. And at a certain point, I had to grow up and say, "It doesn't matter what I want to do. I have to feed people."

What makes me a bold spirit is that I've continuously assessed my life and encouraged myself, "Yes, I have to feed people, but it doesn't mean I have to ignore that calling to build connections that I feel." I've tried many different ways to build connections in community, to reclaim connections of my own. And it doesn't always go as planned. It rarely goes as planned, but I keep trying, and I keep trying to find different ways.

Working in the end-of-life realm has provided me more connection over the last few years than anything else I've done in my life. And it's brought me back to community more than anything else I've ever done. So it's not learning my language. It's not learning to bead or the history of my community. It's not those things. It's being a human being, helping other human beings. I'm really grateful that I was bold enough to keep trying and bold enough to keep making mistakes until I figured it out—not that I have! The work continues.

What is the boldest thing you've done as an end-of-life practitioner?

The boldest thing I did was putting myself out there as a death worker with zero experience. I made up my mind because it clicked, and I just went for it. And at the very beginning, I completely kept it at the forefront. "I am learning and I am a beginner." And to this day, my main work hasn't been holding people's hands at the end of life. It's been supporting other people to support those that are holding those hands at the end of life. And so, as an end-of-life practitioner, that bold spirit, it's definitely just dipping my toe in this pool in the first place.

There was nothing to go on. There was no Indigenous stuff to check out, and I had to crack things wide open.

Today as an end-of-life practitioner, I want . . .

. . . to create lasting, accessible training grounded in culture for Indigenous caregivers.

If that's all I do with all of this, I will be very happy. That's what I want to see happen.

ಸ ಲ

Chrystal Wàban

Chrystal Wàban is a Pikwakanagan First Nation matriarch, wife, Indigenous Counselor, Spiritual Practitioner, and Entrepreneur. Utilizing decades of lived and grassroots work experiences with cultural education, decolonization, and Indigenization, Chrystal operates a social enterprise and community practice known as Blackbird Medicines and the Indigenous Death Doula Collective.

Contact information:

Please contact blackbirdmedicines@gmail.com for collaborative and creative inquiries.

blackbirdmedicines@gmail.com
www.blackbirdmedicines.ca

Book Recommended by Chrystal Waban

Life Stages and Native Women: Memory, Teachings, and Story Medicine
by Kim Anderson and Maria Campbell (2011)

This book inspired me because it gave me a glimpse into the teachings and care I might have grown up with had colonization not occurred. So many grieve the loss of a traditional village, and this book helped me to understand the grief I felt over this in a way that acknowledged the depth and intensity of grief felt over the absence of community. This loss is profound and has historical impacts on Indigenous families and their wellness.

About the Book

"Life Stages and Native Women explores how life stages and responsibilities of Métis, Cree, and Anishinaabe women were integral to the health and well-being of their communities during the mid- 20th century. The book is rich with oral history conducted with fourteen Algonquian elders from the Canadian prairies and Ontario. These elders share stories about the girls and women of their childhood communities at mid-century (1930–1960), and customs related to pregnancy, birth and post-natal care, infant and child care, puberty rites, gender, and age-specific work roles, the distinct roles of post-menopausal women, and women's roles in managing death. The book concludes with a consideration of how oral historians' memories can be applied to building healthier communities today. It is a fascinating and powerful book that will speak to all women." ~ Amazon

CHAPTER 3

PUTTING ON THE BRAKES

"A man's error is his portal to success."

~ James Joyce

"Unit 3299, code 4 for generally unwell." It was the theme for the day, our fifth or sixth call for the exact same thing, and most ended up not being transported to the emergency department. "Generally unwell" is a call type used by the dispatch algorithms when the stated complaint by the 911 caller is vague or includes multiple symptoms. The caller was not feeling well and calling 911, concerned they had COVID-19. Not sure what to do, they called 911.

In most cases, we were being met at the door by someone looking completely fine, stating they had a cough and wanting us to test them for COVID. In the same sentence, they said they knew it wasn't an emergency, didn't need, or wanted to go to the emergency department but wanted us to test them for COVID. We would explain we didn't do COVID testing on the ambulances and often directed the caller to a local assessment center, calling their family physician or the COVID Public Health Line. It was early April, COVID-19 had just started, and no one really understood it, nor how to respond. The province was shutting down, and only essential services, like us, were operating.

Arriving on the scene, we had expectations for a routine call. Only this time, the call would be anything but routine. It would challenge our creative thinking, utilize some of our new palliative care training, and end up taking an unheard-of almost two hours on scene time to end in canceled transportation.

The patient was a ninety-year-old male, recently diagnosed with end-stage cancer, really end-stage—diagnosed one month earlier and expected to die in the next two weeks. He and the family decided to leave the hospital and return home. The family felt prepared, and the care they took in setting up the living room for his make-shift bedroom kept him front and center in family life and provided the comforts and care he needed in his final days.

Everything was set up in their open concept living room. His hospital bed was along one wall next to a picture window looking out over a lovely garden. Another smaller bed, likely for his wife, was tucked beside it. Pictures of the two of them and their daughter sat on shelves near the patient's bedside. Neither the husband nor his wife of seventy years spoke any English, so the daughter translated for everyone. The daughter had no medical training, was currently working full time, at least until her office shut for COVID. She was their only daughter and lived on her own a little ways away.

The patient had not left his bed since arriving one week earlier. His wife tended to all his needs—bathing, feeding, dressing (he insisted on wearing regular clothes in the day and night clothes at night) and toileting with little support needed from the daughter. Prior to his most recent hospital stay, he was mobile using a walker. He went into the hospital after becoming short of breath and was initially treated for pneumonia. He was in his bed on our arrival, a nasal cannula giving him supplement oxygen and a small oxygen delivery machine humming at the foot of his bed.

The daughter explained that over the past few days, her father had stopped caring about dressing, ate less and less even though everything made was his favorite foods, and today he refused any water. The wife stated he slept most of the time and had trouble focusing and holding a conversation with her. The daughter, who didn't live with the couple, came over daily to assist her mother with the care and often found her mother crying softly, holding her father's hand while he slept. Today they called 911 because he was less responsive, more confused when awake, and a couple of times seemed to breathe loudly.

The daughter explained none of the three expected it to be so difficult. The daughter expected her father wouldn't make it to the weekend, and while her mother understood the end was near, she still struggled with the idea of losing her soul-mate. The family had decided it was best to return to the hospital where the proper supports existed to ease the transition for everyone and called 911 to have him transferred. This would normally be a good plan, except we were in a full pandemic, COVID-19, and no visitors were allowed anywhere in the hospital.

Normally our role is to quickly assess, stabilize and transport our patient getting off the scene, usually in about twenty minutes. Our training as paramedics is for emergency lifesaving care and getting the patient to the care they need—in hospital. What we needed on this call was far outside our typical role as paramedics. Fortunately, our service had been selected for a new palliative care initiative from the federal government. Five thousand paramedics across the country were designated to receive this new training. This program would provide paramedics with alternative options, including in-home/non-transport options for patients who had life-limiting, debilitating illnesses and needing urgent medical assistance. We had just started the training for it when COVID-19 struck, halting the program implementation. Despite this, my partner and I realized we needed to use some of the new lessons we had just started to learn.

This call being anything but normal, I realized we needed to hit the brakes and slow things down immensely! Not the normal approach to our hurry-up-and-get-going requests for assistance. While I explained to the daughter there was no rush, and we could take all the time we needed to help her understand the options,[1] my

---

[1] Needs of the Dying #6

partner called our dispatchers to explain we were going to be a while figuring things out, much longer than our traditional twenty-minute response time.

The patient had not been enrolled in any palliative care program yet. The daughter explained plans were in place, but nothing had been discussed other than his wish to die at home with his family beside him. There was no Expected Death in the Home (EDITH) folder to help us connect to his assigned palliative care team and no signed Do Not Resuscitate (DNR) order. The appointment for all this was still being set up by the hospital. The only physician assisting the family was their family physician, who was unreachable.

Sitting outside with the daughter, we discussed the family's needs[23]—to be with their father/husband when he died, for him to die peacefully and comfortably, for the daughter/wife to be supported and be present when he did die. The traditional options to the family and the ones we learned about in our training had changed due to COVID.

The daughter and wife were shocked and dismayed the new hospital no-visitor rule also applied to the palliative care floor.[4] Knowing they wouldn't be allowed in, even just the wife, they struggled with what to do—how to balance the patient's dying wish to pass with his family around him and their struggle with managing the distress of watching his suffering. The decision was made to

---

[2] Needs of the Dying #1
[3] Needs of the Dying #6
[4] Needs of the Dying #8

honor his last wishes, and this brought on a new struggle—what to do when he did die.

The daughter understood calling 911 would result in fire, police, and paramedics all rushing in to "save a life." She didn't want her mother to watch as paramedics and fire personnel did CPR, start IVs, put a tube down her father's throat in a hopeless effort to save his life. But she didn't know what else to do, who else to call. She didn't have a DNR order, and without it, her fears were exactly what would happen.

I placed a call to our local palliative care floor at the hospital.[5] Several phone transfers later, I was speaking with an on-call supervisor. The supervisor and I spoke about the situation, including COVID's impact on services available, the expectations of the family, and options available from both the paramedics and the palliative care unit. The daughter and supervisor also spoke about these options.

The on-call supervisor arranged for a palliative care nurse to come out within the next twenty-four hours and initiate palliative care support for the family. The nurse would bring the EDITH envelope, complete the DNR form and explain the process to follow when the patient finally died. The nurse would also train the daughter in the use of the palliative care symptom assist kit used in our community.[6]

We still had a problem—what if the patient died before these things were in place, especially the DNR? The daughter's fear was either of them—herself or her mother— may, in the distress of the moment, pick up the phone and make the call, only to realize

---

[5] Needs of the Dying #6
[6] Needs of the Dying #7

as paramedics pulled up in full lights and sirens, the call should not have been made. I shared with her that paramedics can call their supervising physician for a Cease Resuscitation Order upon the request of the family and suggested she meet the first responders outside, explain the situation and ask for the call to be made. From my experiences, this works well and avoids the distress of watching what an unwanted resuscitation can create.

The daughter and wife had a plan now, one that honored both the patient's needs and their own.[7] [8] We left the family at home, knowing the nurse would be arriving within the day. We let the family know to call back should they need us; it may not be the two of us responding, but they now had the tools to help the next crew meet the family's needs. We explained to the daughter that we were on shift for the next couple of days and if we heard the call go out for their address, if possible, we would respond. We also notified our supervisor of the situation so he could assist if needed. We didn't hear anything, and as is typical for our field, we don't know the outcome. We assume the patient passed away and hope it was peaceful and at home. Both of us spoke about the call over the next couple of days, the lessons learned, and the strategies we used. We were both content with our actions and felt we did our best for the family in a difficult time.

In September of 2019, York Paramedic Services became one of ten services across Canada to be selected for a new initiative inpatient care and treatment in palliative care. Traditionally most of these patients, after calling 911, are transported to the emergency department where they are exposed to other illnesses and infections their weakened immune systems can't tolerate. Most of the time,

---

[7] Needs of the Dying #14
[8] Needs of the Dying #15

these patients could be safely treated in their homes, avoiding this risk, but the current pre-hospital care system didn't provide that until now. Paramedic services in the new pilot are provided with unique end-of-life training and given new medical directives to support and ease the symptoms these patients have along with the authority to leave the patient at home if appropriate to do so. The training focuses on altering the traditional paramedic approach to a call to respect the needs of the patient who is palliative; it provides more in-depth knowledge and understanding of life-limiting conditions and gives the paramedics alternative treatment options other than simply transporting the emergency department. The goal is to provide access to urgent palliative care when patients need it and where they want it, improving comfort and quality of life for those with debilitating illnesses and their families. The training started in October 2019, and in March 2020, COVID stopped all in-person training, effectively halting the implementation of the new protocols and directives. The expectation is the program will be restarted once the current pandemic is better under control. Until then, as demonstrated in this case, paramedics are using the initial lessons learned to the benefit of their patients and families.

Changing the mentality of a group of people is never an easy task. For a paramedic, the mental approach to managing a palliative care call is very different from the emergency care call for which we spend years training where we aim to keep the patient alive, to stabilize and treat their condition with the hopes of making them better, and quickly get them to the hospital for definitive care. In palliative care, we aren't trying to make them better or heal them; we are instead working to make them more comfortable and ease their current distress. We aren't going to fix them or their condition, but we can make the current situation better for them. This change in focus or mentality is a big shift to make. This is especially challenging when the paramedic needs to be able to adjust at a moment's notice. We don't know arriving on a scene if the call will need our "emergency care mentality" or "palliative care mentality." It is not until we walk through the door and sort through the details the family or patient provides us with do we know it's time to hit the brakes and shift our mindset. The best example is the speed of the call. In regular 911 calls, our mindset is quick, accurate, efficient decisions aimed at getting off the scene and en-route to the hospital quickly. Time is considered heart and brain muscle, so paramedics must be fast thinkers and movers. In a palliative care 911 call, time can be slowed down, and often the most appropriate solution isn't always obvious. Family and even the patient may not know what they need to tell us to help us help them, so it is up to the paramedic to slow things down, take the time, and put together the more complicated pieces of the puzzle. Paramedics aren't trained to sit and chat, take their time; they are taught to get up and move.

This call could have gone very differently if we had acted as "normal paramedics." Taking the patient to the hospital is never really seen as a wrong decision, except in this case. We were concerned that should we take the patient to the hospital, it would have been via the Emergency Department (ED). He would have been on a hospital stretcher, likely in the hall waiting hours, as the main reason for the transfer wasn't to fix anything; it was to assist the family in coping with the end of life. Either he would have been admitted to the ED or if room existed possibly to the palliative care floor, or he would have been discharged back home to wait for a bed on the palliative care floor. Either way, his family would not have been allowed into the hospital to be with him, and he could have very likely passed away in a foreign hospital room without his family around.[9] Instead, he stayed at home, and his family had the supports coming into place with an interim plan until those supports arrived.

Student paramedics sometimes ask me, "What do you do when there is nothing you can do for a patient?" My response is there is always something we can do, even if only being there is the only option. In this call, we didn't do any traditional "paramedical" lifesaving skills, but the ones we did use are just as valuable to the patient, their family, and the paramedics on the call.

℘ ℆

Addressing the Needs of the Dying

Taking the time to sit with the family and learn what they needed; treated the father as a living person; gave the family the knowledge they needed to make decisions appropriate for them and the support they needed to feel less alone and overwhelmed in the final days.

Connecting the family with the palliative care team provided the family with the tools, resources, and supports they needed to help decrease emotional, physical, and mental pain, hopefully making his passing more peaceful and dignified

℘ ℆

---

[9] Needs of the Dying #15

A self-care tip

Find something that makes you feel good about yourself or makes you feel special and appreciated, then practice it on a regular basis.

One tip or strategy to help other caregivers

Know your boundaries and honor them; they are protective and help you be your best for them.

Something I wish I had known when I began

End-of-life care is very new to our field, and our field doesn't allow for a lot of outside-the-box thinking unless the field is ready for it. We are bound by very rigid protocols/procedures.

There is knowledge I wish I had in the earlier years in my career; however, at the same time, this knowledge I have now and my different approach isn't something that would have been supported then. It is only due to the change in the landscape of our field that we are even now able to consider some of these different approaches; even still, earlier in my career, I wasn't seasoned enough to appreciate the knowledge and use it appropriately

℘ ℭ

Shannon Koppenhoefer

Shannon is a twenty-one-year Paramedic, an Advanced Care Paramedic who is passionate about expanding the role paramedics have in the healthcare system, specifically in the pre-hospital scene. As a Community Paramedic, she helps improve healthcare system navigation by connecting 911 callers to appropriate social and health services, providing vaccinations at community clinics, and working with vulnerable, at-risk, or chronically ill residents to decrease their reliance on the 911 system. Shannon has been recognized by her peers twice for her dedication to the community with the Community Awareness and Contribution Award. She is a recipient of the Distinguished Service Medal for Paramedics, recognizing her achievements and contributions to paramedicine. Shannon has been published in the Canadian Paramedicine publication. Shannon holds a Bachelor of Science, Physician Assistant Degree from the University of Toronto School of Community Medicine.

Contact information:

Website: www.artraining.on.ca
Email: shannon@artraining.on.ca

Book Recommended by Shannon Koppenhoefer

Into Thin Air
by Jon Krakauer (1999)

The main character trained hard, overcame obstacles and started his climb to Everest. The book was more about the journey to deciding what you are capable of and what you are willing to do to be the best you can be by your own definitions—not those of others. It used the preparation and actual Everest Climb as a metaphor, which is all I will say so as not to spoil it for others. I read the book when I was just starting out as an adult, after graduating university and looking at career and life as an adult for the first time. It inspired me to possibilities and to see the path to those possibilities differently—with more optimism and energy than I had known. The storyline wasn't the trigger, but the message creatively woven into the storyline was. It energized me and gave me confidence at a time in my life when so much was up in the air, changing and uncertain.

About the Book

"A bank of clouds was assembling on the not-so-distant horizon, but journalist-mountaineer Jon Krakauer, standing on the summit of Mt. Everest, saw nothing that 'suggested that a murderous storm was bearing down.' He was wrong. The storm, which claimed five lives and left countless more--including Krakauer's--in guilt-ridden disarray, would also provide the impetus for Into Thin Air, Krakauer's epic account of the May 1996 disaster." ~ Amazon

CHAPTER 4

SERENITY AND MINDFULNESS

"To care for those who once cared for us is
one of the highest honors."

~ Tia Walker

"Les, this week, the doctors used a word that they have never used before." I froze. Somehow, I already knew what he was going to say. He said the word, but he didn't have to. Over the years, we had made such a connection, enjoyed deep conversations, and my intuition knew what he wanted to say. His voice wavered as he cleared his throat. His cancer was *terminal*.[10]

After over five years of many surgeries, dozens of chemotherapy sessions, and multiple radiation treatments, the reality of "no cure for this cancer" reared its ugly head.

On a sunny afternoon in September, I relaxed with my dear friend in my living room, listening to his favorite music while setting up a new media console with an electric fireplace. He was on the rug facing the wall, so his back was to me when I heard him express his worst fears. I moved closer, knelt behind him, but could not look him in the eyes, and something told me it was the right decision.

Me: Stop and take a break.

Him: No, Les. It's okay. I want to do this. It's easy for me.[11]

Perhaps this is a good distraction for him. I had many questions, in true Lesley fashion, but I bit my lip. "What can I do to support you?" I finally asked.

Him: My daughters. Please keep an eye on my girls. You are not the only one I am asking. I just about broke down, but I was determined to be strong—for him.

Me: I'm honored. Of course, I will do my best. But please. Stop now. Do you want to talk about your last appointment?

---

[10] Needs of the Dying #4
[11] Needs of the Dying #4

Him: There's nothing to say. The trial chemotherapy was working, but now the cancer's back and has spread.

I gently put my arms around him, gave him a long, gentle squeeze, and kissed the back of his neck while remaining still for a short while. I liked that we were kindred spirits, and I loved him unconditionally.[12] My mind was racing. I HATE CANCER! I was fighting back the tears. It's not fair. My friend was one of the most amazing people on this earth, very fit and active, never smoked, and took care of his body. He never, ever complained. Yet, he was cursed with the rarest of the rarest form of thyroid cancer.

Him: Look, see. I'm done. He tested both power switches, and, as expected, the unit worked perfectly.

Me: Why don't you go relax in the backyard, and I will join you soon.

He nodded. I didn't want to leave him alone, but I needed a minute to compose myself. I needed to listen with my heart, not my head, and respect that he didn't want to talk about it.[13] Sometimes silence is golden. A teacher once told me that the words *listen* and *silent* are spelled with the same letters. I finally understood why.

As I joined him outside, there was a slight chill, and under the blue sky, he had fallen sound asleep in the hammock. This was the last time I would see him in my backyard.

---

[12] Needs of the Dying #5
[13] Needs of the Dying #4

> **"Sometimes the hardest thing about holding space is it can feel and look a lot like doing nothing."**
> ~ **Heather Plett**

Early December, out of character, I received within a minute both an urgent text and also a phone call, and my friend said, "Lesley, I need a favor." I could sense that he needed my help. When I arrived at his house, I was a bit shocked. He was sitting, unshaven, in the kitchen with his mom and didn't look very well. He had a towel over his head and asked me to go to the pharmacy and pick up a prescription.[14]

Once I arrived at his home, I sat with him and asked if I could stay; I just didn't feel right leaving them as he was getting weaker and his mom needed respite. I set up a sleeping area on the floor beside his bed. The next morning, I encouraged him to call his doctor; it had been a bad night for him. He was in serious pain, and moving took every ounce of energy that he had. I was conflicted, as I had to work, but deep down, I wanted to stay and take care of him.[15] He promised he would call the doctor who ordered tests. A couple of days later, the scan showed that a growth on his spine was in such a place that it impacted his mobility. The doctors presented two options: 1) do nothing, or 2) have spinal surgery, which came with risks. He chose surgery as he could bear the pain no more, and he simply was not yet ready to stop living.[16] The surgery was scheduled, and I drove his mom down so that we could see him before. We were allowed down with him just prior

---

[14] Needs of the Dying #13
[15] Needs of the Dying #6
[16] Needs of the Dying #5

to entering the operating room. It was hard to let go of his hand and my hug.[17]

His mom had brought a thermos of homemade soup—her expression of love. The waiting room was only half-full, and we tried to close our eyes while we sat upright in the chairs. I noticed a room labeled "family." I was relieved that his mom was able to lay down on the couch using her hat and scarf as a pillow. I pushed two chairs together for me, and that was sufficient. The room was dark, quiet and we were able to sleep for a couple of hours. A nurse in green scrubs came with the news that the surgery was over and they would be monitoring him in the recovery room. Even though it was after midnight, his mom asked me to call and text a few people to let them know he was okay.

A long while later, we were told we could see him in the Intensive Care Unit (ICU). What I saw scared me as he suddenly looked much older than fifty-one. All those machines! His eyes were closed, and I was concerned when I saw him wearing an oxygen mask. The nurse must have seen our worried faces and reassured us that this was normal and that his vital signs were stable. We stayed a short while so that she could rub his feet and carefully put on his favorite socks as only a mom could. I held his hand, and we paused for another prayer that he would have a full recovery. I didn't want to leave him alone.[18]

It was after two in the morning, and it was another bitterly cold night, and after taking his mom home, it was almost 4 a.m., I realized I was exhausted, and yet I had work in the morning. I was annoyed that my job was so busy, and I was hesitant to ask for time

---

[17] Needs of the Dying #6
[18] Needs of the Dying #3

off, which was reserved for immediate family. The weekend couldn't come fast enough, and I headed to the hospital for a good long visit. Thankfully, he was now out of the ICU and given a room to himself. He was sleeping when I arrived, so I quietly pulled up a chair and just sat and looked at him. I wanted to hold his hand, but I didn't want to wake him. In fact, if the bed had been wider, I would have crawled in beside him.[19] It's almost as if he heard my thoughts as he opened his eyes. He was surprised to see me, and I could tell he was a bit groggy.

Me: What can I do to comfort you?

Him: Cloth. My head.[20]

I brought the cool, damp washcloth and gently positioned it on his forehead. He moved his hand and adjusted it so slightly, and then a slight smile and a wink. I was hopeful it provided some pain relief.[21] I reached for his closest hand and softly caressed the back of his hand and arm.

Him: You don't have to stay.

Me: I want to be here with you.

He relaxed. Around the room, I saw a small decorated Christmas tree with ornament photos of young relatives, signs of his step-daughter, step-son, and other visitors. The man who refused any family or friends to escort him to any doctor's appointments or medical procedures at the hospital finally

---

[19] Needs of the Dying #1
[20] Needs of the Dying #11
[21] Needs of the Dying #11

welcomed someone by his side. The nurse came to attend to him, so I respected his privacy[22] and took a walk outside just to get a bit of fresh air. No use, it was freezing cold, so I headed back in.

I had brought some body lotion, warmed some up in my hands before giving him a foot massage. I tried to hold my sadness in; doing this little thing to help him brought me joy. He drifted back to sleep.[23] With the intravenous (IV) sound going *drip, drip, drip,* soon several hours passed, and while I didn't want to leave him, it was getting dark. As if on cue, his dad walked in. We didn't need to exchange words, just smiles and nods. And then I left to give his dad private time with his son.

A few days later, he was discharged and sent home; he wanted to be surrounded by family,[24] and there wasn't a hospice in his region. When I phoned his mom, I could tell she was happy her baby was coming home but that she wasn't prepared for all the activity and medical equipment that was needed for palliative care.[25] She had some help rearranging the furniture to make room for a hospital bed, in the ideal position, so that he could still watch sports and movies on TV. But there were other unfamiliar and somewhat daunting items: the wheelchair, the IV stand, the commode, the urinal, and the Hoyer lift. He was now on a feeding tube and a pain pump. There was chaos with staff coming and going from various homecare organizations—a nurse, a personal support worker, an occupational therapist, a doctor. The phone and doorbell kept ringing with deliveries of medical supplies. I had avoided talking about the wound on his thyroid, which was now as large on the

---

[22] Needs of the Dying #14
[23] Needs of the Dying #6
[24] Needs of the Dying #5
[25] Needs of the Dying #7

outside as it was on the inside. He was given a suction machine for removing saliva from his mouth.[26]

He had an upcoming appointment with the oncologist and requested all the family attend with him.[27] This was unprecedented as in all the years for the multiple surgeries, treatments, and doctor visits, he insisted on going alone, even if it meant taking two buses and the subway.

There were ten of us in the room: his parents, his two daughters, his brother and sister-in-law, his cousin and best friend, and me.[28] We maintained a sense of hope for good news and the next steps.[29] His oncologist took a double-take when she opened the door as she expected to see only him, as with all his previous appointments.

I was seated beside his wheelchair as we listened to the prognosis. None of us liked what we heard, but the words that came out of the specialist's mouth brought the needed credibility. If anyone in the room had any doubts, this moment revealed that our beautiful soul was dying and did not have much longer to live.[30] You could feel the tension in the room. I wanted to run away. I heard sobs from the women in the room. The men were emotional but were able to control their tears. I did not want to be there. I asked a silly question and felt embarrassed. I wanted a different answer. This was not fair. I was angry at the world. The appointment ended on a bitter note, and I called for the transport

---

[26] Needs of the Dying #13
[27] Needs of the Dying #5
[28] Needs of the Dying #12
[29] Needs of the Dying #2
[30] Needs of the Dying #8

service to pick us up. It was rush hour, and unlike the morning pick-up time, which was planned, we had to wait. My patience was running thin. Everything for the rest of the day was all wrong. *Why was it so cold? Is he in pain? Why was it taking so long? Is he hungry? Why does cancer even exist? Why does he have to suffer?*[31] And it was so cold outside, with a long, cold drive home. I was ashamed of my feelings, my words, and my actions.

My friend was such a considerate and caring person that he even protected others as he was dying. He was determined to enjoy a final Christmas with his family at the beautiful home of his brother and sister-in-law. That year, I was honored to spend New Year's Eve on the couch right beside him[32] to give his mom a much-needed rest. I regularly checked on him, his pain pump, ensuring his mouth and airway were clear, and topped up the IV bag with the nutrition drink for his feeding tube.[33]

A couple of days into the new year, there was a medical emergency with uncontrolled bleeding from the cancerous wound on his neck. His mom was home alone with him, so she phoned 911, and he was taken to the closest local hospital by ambulance. After they stabilized him, they took him to the hospital where his specialist worked. He was now unable to breathe on his own due to a blockage in his airway. Over the next few days, there was an outpouring of family and friends who visited him.[34]

---

[31] Needs of the Dying #6
[32] Needs of the Dying #1
[33] Needs of the Dying #10
[34] Needs of the Dying #13

Although he was on a rapid decline,[35] he held on to see his elder daughter's birthday[36] (two days before he died) and also his mom's birthday (the day before he died). On that fateful evening, I was at the hospital with his mom, and there were signs of distress. He was pulling at the breathing tube, and at one point, he opened his eyes quite large and looked directly at me. Despite being so weak, his arms were so strong that we each held his hands to calm him.[37] His dad arrived, followed by his brother and sister-in-law, so I decided to give the family some time alone. I stepped out of the room to call and update his best friend, who spent the entire day before by his side. I couldn't have been gone more than ten minutes when his sister-in-law texted me, "He's gone."

I sensed that he was even protecting his daughters and me as we were not there to witness him take his last breath. It was comforting to know he died with peace and dignity, surrounded by loved ones.[38] [39]

> "Love is always bestowed as a gift - freely, willingly and without expectation. We don't love to be loved; we love to love."
>
> ~ Leo Buscaglia

The funeral director assured the family that the staff would exhibit utmost respect for his body during the transportation,

---

[35] Needs of the Dying #13
[36] Needs of the Dying #12
[37] Needs of the Dying #13
[38] Needs of the Dying #15
[39] Needs of the Dying #14

dressing, and embalming process.⁴⁰ The viewing was ten days after his death, and visitors came from out of town, out of province, and out of the country to offer support and sympathy to his family. It was an open casket, and he lay peacefully, looking more handsome than his twin, Denzel Washington.

It was standing room only at the church the next day for his funeral, and I was honored to perform a reading. After the funeral, there was a lovely reception at the funeral home, courtesy of his sister-in-law's parents. There was not a dry eye after the speeches, tributes; even his younger daughter read a very touching piece from her heart.⁴¹

The family invited me to his cremation ceremony. I use the word ceremony, as I see rituals as important in the grief journey after the death of a loved one. It was a privilege to accompany them and bear witness as he transitioned from his physical body to a place beyond.⁴²

It was a noticeably cold, gloomy day in mid-January, and we met at the small inconspicuous outside building hidden amongst the trees. What a stark contrast to the beautiful funeral home where the visitation was held just days prior. The container in which he laid was gently placed⁴³ into a specially designed furnace, called a retort or cremation chamber. As a person who has a tremendous fear of fire, I became very anxious. But I remembered that although temperatures can get up to 1,000°C, his body would not actively be

---

⁴⁰ Needs of the Dying #16
⁴¹ Needs of the Dying #12
⁴² Needs of the Dying #16
⁴³ Needs of the Dying #16

set on fire. Instead, the intense heat of the flames would reduce his body to gases and bone fragments over two to four hours.

Six people were allowed to attend the viewing: his mother, his father, his sister-in-law, a close family friend, his best friend, and me. The attending staff asked if anyone had wanted to press the button to initiate the process. The tears were pouring down my face when I saw his mom boldly step forward without hesitation say, "I brought my son into this world, and I will be the one to send him off."

My mind drifted, and I realized how much this situation resembled her prized sunflower garden at the front of her house. Each year, she religiously planted the seeds and welcomed their brilliant yellow hues and large blooms. She lovingly cared for them, tended to the soil, and ensured adequate water, supporting any weaker ones as needed. The affection she had, especially for her children and grandchildren, ensured they thrived. Just as she was proud of her family, her garden was admired by the entire neighborhood; understandable as sunflowers are warm, happy, bright, and cheerful. It's a flower that represents loyalty as it always follows the sun with a desire to seek light and truth. The energy ignited by the heat and flames reminded me of my friend standing tall and strong, so resilient to his health challenges, and radiating everlasting love. It is fitting that sunflower seeds were his favorite snack.

Some believe that on cloudy days when the sun is not shining, sunflowers share energy by facing each other. Whether or not this is fact or myth, this sentiment felt true as we stood in this dimly lit structure. Yes, it was a somber time, but we were providing warmth, comfort, and sharing each other's strength as we huddled closely together. We need each other's support in the darkest of times, especially when grieving the loss of a loved one. And once again, I fulfilled the promise of not leaving him alone.

Being present until the final point in time when he was with us physically created such a meaningful experience for me. It was an immensely sad moment, and I felt a sense of calm, understanding that the cremation was a painless and peaceful process.[44] We stayed less than an hour, and as we parted ways, I looked back. His best friend, an avid photographer, took a photo. Our profound loss was marked by smoke exiting the chimney of this little house that would be our friend's home for the next few hours.

"Forever in our hearts and memories."
~ Unknown

I didn't leave my house for about two weeks after the cremation. Working from home, I was just going through the motions and didn't want to return phone calls of people checking in on me. Some days, I didn't shower, couldn't remember if I had eaten, and I went into a state of depression. I ordered groceries online, but I had lost my appetite. I slept a lot. He was often in my dreams. I cried so much and produced so many tears that I developed a painful stye on my eye. One good thing was that I kept hydrated by drinking lots of water and tea.

---

[44] Needs of the Dying #16

I reflected on an evening a few years prior when we walked down by the lake on the beach admiring the orange sunset. He was in remission at this time, and our conversation led to me saying, "I don't want to die alone." As always, he had a positive response and encouraged me to adjust my mindset to "I don't want to live alone." He lived life fully,[45] and I realized I wasn't. At that moment, I changed.

It dawned on me that for months, he must have been doing the daunting task of preparing for his own death, and yet at no point did I see him depressed or anxious. I think he accomplished the really hard emotional work of going deep to a place of peace and acceptance. Maybe he was looking forward to a profoundly spiritual experience and reconciling with God in life after death.[46] Perhaps he worried that he wouldn't be there to provide for his family, wanting reassurance that all would be OK after he died.

"The best and most beautiful things in the world cannot be seen or even touched - they must be felt with the heart."

~ Helen Keller

The Catholic Church allows cremation, but the ashes cannot be separated and must be laid to rest in a sacred space as soon as possible. His mom had a special place at home for his ashes

---

[45] Needs of the Dying #4
[46] Needs of the Dying #9

where she, his daughters, his sister, and the rest of the family could easily speak words of love.[47] [48]

A date in June was selected for the interment when close family and friends met at the cemetery. We were fortunate it was not raining, and the ground was dry. During the rite of committal, the priest offered prayers beside the small open grave prior to committing his remains to his final resting place.[49]

His sister-in-law played "Tears in Heaven" by Eric Clapton from her phone, and as I listened, I was comforted to observe that he would be placed underneath a large tree, the roots of which gave stability. It was a perfect location, shaded, near a bench in the cemetery and close to the road. He loved being in nature, and the smell of the cool soil made me feel grounded, content, and trusting that this was exactly where he was meant to be.

We took turns placing earth; some used the shovel while others used their hands. This action united us, provided a sense of closure, and was a sign of respect for his final goodbye. His mom placed flowers, the first of many that the family and friends would bring on their future visits to beautify his resting place.[50]

It was lunchtime, and we made our way to the nearby restaurant where we had a private area reserved. The variety of scents from the fresh vegetables to hot wings and ribs to the red wine – there was something for everyone, and we welcomed the nourishment.

---

[47] Needs of the Dying #12
[48] Needs of the Dying #16
[49] Needs of the Dying #16
[50] Needs of the Dying #16

The opportunity to support my friend and his family through his end-of-life journey was a true gift. It was a humbling experience to serve in such meaningful ways, and I know I have found my purpose. For me, everything starts at my heart, and I need to embrace the beauty in life in order to continually heal. Grief exists, but I allow room for gratitude that he is no longer suffering.

After the joyful gathering at the restaurant, I was anticipating remembering him in my unique way whenever I miss him. Although it was summer, I sat comfortably in my living room, his photo in view, turned on my faux fireplace, and listened to some of his favorite songs. The serenity of the day and the current moment of solitude brought me balance, and I was happy that I had started this tradition and kept my promise of never leaving him alone.

**Hold on to what is good even if it is
a handful of earth.
Hold on to what you believe even if it is
a tree which stands by itself.
Hold on to what you must do even if it is
a long way from here.
Hold on to life even when it is
easier letting go.
Hold on to my hand even when I have
gone away from you.**

~ Many Winters, Nancy Wood

When my friend was dying, I was described by others as a very compassionate person. For me, being compassionate is part of who I am. It's not only a beautiful personal trait, but compassion enabled me to love him unconditionally. I was able to look past the disease and see him for the person he was and what he meant to so many—father, son, brother, uncle, nephew, friend.

I made it a choice to be mindful and sensitive to the suffering, pain, and grief experienced by my friend and his loved ones. I could sense his discomfort and had the intuition to act in ways to provide comfort, even if it meant sitting in silence.

In addition to being sensitive, I tried to be sensible while providing support while he was dying. I consider myself resourceful and used the knowledge and wisdom I acquired at work about the health care system in Ontario to know what services were available.

ೞ ಐ

What was taboo

I was a friend, not family. In the hospital, I had questions and asked different nurses, but because I was not related to the patient, they could not answer me. I respect the privacy laws of personal health information. He was my soulmate, so it was frustrating, and not knowing created more fear. The reality was that talking about death was taboo. If I really wanted specifics about certain signs of decline, I could have approached the family or done research online. At times, I was scared and was craving for answers, so I believe wisdom reduces fear.

Resources I tapped into

Friends: My high school friends were going through their own grief journeys, and I am thankful for the many text messages and updates and group chats. In a sense, we were each other's "grief buddy" as we individually had our relationship with our special friend, who we had known for over thirty-five years.

Counseling: I tapped into professional counseling to help address the painful grief I was experiencing. I am fortunate for the Employee Assistance Program (EAP) offered at my work. Sometimes, talking to a far-removed expert can provide strategies for healing.

Family: I am thankful for my close-knit family. My sisters and parents, and children reminded me to do self-care. Whether attending the visitation, the funeral, or offering loving words, I appreciated their love and support and truly believe that love lessens grief.

Moment of revelation

> **"Grief is the price we pay for love."**
> **~ Queen Elizabeth II**

I was grieving immensely because I loved my friend so deeply. We do not get over our grief; we must work through it. Loss brings grief and emotions. It's important to recognize our feelings and reflect. I learned that I experienced disenfranchised grief, or hidden grief, which is sometimes unacknowledged or invalidated. I was holding in my feelings which was not healthy and manifested physical ailments in my body. I discovered that mourning activities are beneficial and lead to healing. Being a co-author of this book has been an incredible pathway to healing for me.

A self-care tip that helped me

Years ago, I bought a wooden wall decor carved with the word *serenity*. It hangs in my home so that I see it daily. The word, serenity, resonates with me, and I created these self-care tips as an acronym:

Solitude and Silence – find quiet alone time and bring awareness to proper breathing, inhaling, exhaling.
Emotional Balance – be extra focused on managing stress.
Remembering – so important to say his name and cherish the fond memories and significant dates.
Expressive Arts – dance, music, creative writing. Since I do not keep a journal, writing this chapter was healing.
Nourish body, mind, and soul in nature – get outside, listen to guided meditations, practice mindfulness.
Initiate traditions, rituals, and ceremonies – this brings us together in community and reminds us to appreciate.
Talk – find a grief buddy – seek counseling, talk to your doctor, your family, friends, neighbors, colleagues.
You are not alone – find support from the many resources online – podcasts, blogs, books, social media.

Self-care tip for caregivers

Physical self-care: Have a bath. Make time to pamper yourself using this relaxing self-care ritual, at least weekly. Run a warm bath – I add Epsom Salts and soak in the tub: relief for my aches & pains. Instrumental music – no lyrics – turn your mind off and just listen to gentle, soft music. Or nature sounds, guided meditation – check out the Calm app or others. Many are free. Optional: Candles. Dim the lights, close your eyes, or put on an eye cover. I love my diffuser and my collection of essential oils. Lavender is soothing before bed. Hydrate – important to drink water before and after. Moisturize – apply your favorite body lotions or creams. Bedding – Fresh sheets on your bed or clean pajamas and a clean pillowcase. Sleep – Aim to get at least seven hours. This routine helps me sleep like a baby.

Tip or strategy to help other caregivers

Accept help or ask for assistance. You cannot do this alone. If friends or family offer, give them a specific task. Examples: Provide a list of grocery items, ask to pick up a prescription (call the pharmacy to give authorization), walk the dog, load/unload the dishwasher, help with a load of laundry, pick up kids from school or activities, prioritize mail/bills, return phone calls to update others.

Tips for practitioners

When someone is dying, letting go is not to be viewed as a failure or that the person has given up. No one should have to die in pain. This is one of the biggest fears people have: to experience pain at the end of life. Whether it is the last months, weeks, days or hours, end-of-life practitioners need to focus on providing comfort measures. It is important to have early conversations on what would bring comfort to people with terminal illnesses, spiritually, emotionally, and physically. I believe that comfort soothes pain.

The impact on me from this experience

I have found my purpose, my calling. There is intention in everything I do, and my purpose is to love unconditionally. I am right where I need to be, and through advocacy and education, I want to empower others to be comfortable with end-of-life planning conversations. Everything we experience in life teaches us a lesson. I have learned to accept my own mortality and have gained so much knowledge both from experiential learning and traditional academic models. I have a strong desire to share my wisdom with others to help reduce their fears around death, dying, grief and bereavement.

My name is Lesley James. **My core values are** love, wisdom, and comfort. **I believe that** LOVE lessens Grief, WISDOM reduces Fear, and COMFORT soothes Pain.

What I wish I had known when I began on this journey as a practitioner in end-of-life care and what I discovered about it

As I began on my journey as an end-of-life doula, planner, and educator, I wish I had known how significant emotions and grief are connected to death and dying. I acknowledge as an empath that I need to have a support system and dedicate time to self-care.

Caregiver burn-out is so prevalent, and many of us don't even think of ourselves as caregivers, but we are. Sometimes I didn't stick to my boundaries, especially around time commitments. I needed proper rest to properly take care of my friend and provide respite for his mom. Later, I realized the negative impact of over-extending myself. Remembering my own needs for good health was equally important. I could have recommended other resources to the family, such as an end-of-life doula or hospice volunteers. Caregiving takes a village.

༄ ༅

How are end-of-life practitioners bold spirits?

End-of-life practitioners are courageous. They have grown in their compassion and empathy. It's a calling. It's *in* them. They were drawn to do this to serve others and to help others have a better experience at the end of life.

End-of-life practitioners are brave and courageous enough to embrace and empower others to have the conversation around death and dying and grief and bereavement and living what you want and how someone wants to be remembered. Medical staff are trained to save and fix a person, except for in palliative care and hospice. I believe, however, that with COVID, they're getting better, but they're still in hospital to offer treatments, do tests, procedures, smf surgeries to try and make the person better. But with hospice and with any end-of-life practitioner, especially an end-of-life doula, can have more of that consistent one-on-one relationship with their client.

How are caregivers, the non-paid family or friend caregiver, a bold spirit?

I've seen it with my own family. My mom, dad, and uncle provided caregiving for both my grandmothers. Their unconditional love drives caregivers. Tia Walker said, "To care for those who once cared for us is one of the highest honors." I believe that. Caregivers will do anything for their loved ones if and when the time comes. They're driven by love.

What makes the dying person a bold spirit?

I can only imagine the things that are going through their mind. Have I lived my life to the fullest? Who's going to take care of my family? My children? Have I made peace with [whomever]? Is there forgiveness? Are there any things I need to address with anybody to soften the heart and have some tender moments with loved ones?

At the end of life, we're all independent people. Well, there are some that are very overdependent on some people and use them, but for the most part, we like to do stuff ourselves. It's difficult to rely on and really depend on other people when you're used to being independent. After a recent fairly minor surgery, it was hard for me to allow people who wanted to help me, do so. My family wanted to help. I was thinking I was being a burden and I didn't want to be a burden on anyone; I wanted to do things myself. And yet, I had to accept that I had lost the ability to care for myself. It's bold to accept that.

What makes you a bold spirit as an end-of-life practitioner?

What makes me a bold spirit is mindfulness to notice that I need to listen and hear what the dying individual is telling me. Sometimes, it's okay to acknowledge in silence and sit in silence. You don't always have to be constantly saying things, because I think serenity and calmness and just being with the person and maybe they're processing a lot and, if they're not up to talking, you don't have to talk. You can just sit with them. Something that stuck with me a few years ago was when I learned the words listen and silent have the same letters. It just resonates with me that with some people, they can finish each other's sentences. You know what they're thinking, and you don't need to verbalize everything.

It's healthy to express feelings, but when the time comes, sometimes it is just a look or a touch, or there are other ways to bring comfort. You can just turn on some music, bring some flowers, brighten up the room. There are other ways other than always talking to bring comfort. So I'm learning to be more mindful about listening, including listening to body language.

What's the boldest thing you've ever done in end-of-life care?

The boldest thing I've ever done as a non-medical person was for my friend who was in the last couple of weeks of his life, not able to take food by mouth. I learned very quickly how to fill and operate the feeding tube, ensure proper hygiene—bedside caregiving. I realized I had to just do this. He was dependent, and there was no one else to do it. I had to because I was providing respite for his mother.

As an end-of-life practitioner, I want to . . .

. . . empower others not to fear death.

Death is a normal human experience. It can be a sacred, peaceful, beautiful event, and I want people to think about and have conversations about end-of-life care, end-of-life planning and act on it. Family is going to be in a grieving situation with the loss of their loved one; they don't need the extra distress of thinking, "Is this what my loved one would have wanted?" The most beautiful gift is to empower others, give the gift to their loved ones, talk about it, put it in writing, document it, review it, revise it, and communicate your end-of-life wishes because life is short.

༄ ༅

Lesley James (née Mogg)
Licensed Willow EOL Educator™

Lesley is a compassionate End-of-Life Planner, Educator, and Founder of Last Wishes Consulting. In 2020, Lesley became an End-of-Life Doula and completed courses in hospice, palliative care, advance care planning, legacy, green burials, death, dying, grief and bereavement. Lesley works and volunteers in the bereavement sector and is currently a regional co-representative at the Bereavement Ontario Network, supporting the Simcoe-York-Dufferin regions. A Jamaican-born Canadian, she is grateful for the support of her loving family and is an ally to the disability community. She is an active member of several networks and associations, which can be found on her website. In 2021, Lesley completed courses in funeral pre-planning and brings comfort and peace of mind to end-of-life conversations.

Contact information:

Markham, Ontario, Canada
lastwishesconsulting@gmail.com
www.lastwishesconsulting.ca
https://linktr.ee/LastWishesConsulting

Book Recommended by Lesley James

The Wild Edge of Sorrow
by Francis Weller (2015)

This is truly an apprenticeship of sorrow. Until I read this book, I had no idea how much hidden grief I had experienced, not just loss. I had buried it, and it was affecting my life. I learned many things, including the deeper one has loved a person, the more intense the grief and feelings of loss. In addition, I no longer feel guilty if I am thankful in one way (not having to witness the pain and suffering) after a loved one dies. It is okay to hold space for both grief and gratitude at the same time as part of our healing journey. This book also impacted me as now I understand the connection with death and grief.

About the Book

"Noted psychotherapist Francis Weller provides an essential guide for navigating the deep waters of sorrow and loss in this lyrical yet practical handbook for mastering the art of grieving. Describing how Western patterns of amnesia and anesthesia affect our capacity to cope with personal and collective sorrows, Weller reveals the new vitality we may encounter when we welcome, rather than fear, the pain of loss. Through moving personal stories, poetry, and insightful reflections he leads us into the central energy of sorrow, and to the profound healing and heightened communion with each other and our planet that reside alongside it."
~ Amazon

CHAPTER 5

MY BOAT HAS ARRIVED

"The greatest explorer on this earth never takes voyages as long as those of the man who descends to the depth of his heart."

~ Julien Green

On a casual day in November in Kerala, India, my paternal grandmother M. John was not having a good day. When I saw her,

her hair was ungroomed, and her smile had faded. I didn't hesitate to take her to a nearby hospital. She'd been to this hospital before for MRI scans, her hands trembling a bit when she was done with it, explaining, "I heard some boom sounds," and we waited for the report. The duty nurse approached, and I was called into the doctors' room. I remained frozen, trying to understand that she had a tertiary phase malignancy. Then explained, "It's on top of the pancreas." The treatment option was an immediate surgery but with a very low success rate.

Many things came to my mind, and I thought, *Is this real?* I never saw anything unusual about her well-being until the night before. I questioned myself, *Why her again? Such struggle. Her life has been hard.* She'd come to the world with a destiny to live with her mother for only a few days. She regularly said to me, "I didn't get enough mom's milk, so I'm different." And then there was the early passing of our grandfather, a Christian missionary. With my upset face, I approached Grandma, and she questioned me about the results. A feeble voice emanated from me as I told her the whole story.

Her response was somewhat different than I had anticipated. "I have completed my duties on earth," she explained. "I am ready to go for God's call. Christ will carry my sufferings." She didn't tremble at the news and even tried to cheer me up. I could see her firm belief in God as she accepted her disease with a smile.

Accepting disease with a positive attitude is the first thing in overcoming disease! Have you been to a state like this? Will you accept? Not accept? It is up to the person with the terminal illness to determine how they will move forward—either treatment immediately, wait for treatment, or no treatment whatsoever.

My grandma surprised me by telling me she would accept the disease with all its pain and outcome—death. It surprised me because people usually choose treatment in my experience, and in this case, my grandma chose to accept the disease. She was ready to go—to die. In my culture, Indian, that is an acceptable decision because she was eighty-four years old, and when someone is over the age of eighty, it means we are lucky we are still alive. With a terminal illness, we are happy to accept that we will die. If younger, then the individual would typically choose to receive treatment.

Cancer had metastasized, affecting almost all the major organs of her body and a steady decline starting with pronounced weight loss, decrease in appetite, and lack of sleep, the new normal. Frequent pain radiating all through her body was affecting her, especially at night. One night around midnight, she told me, "I can't stand the pain today. I need to go to the hospital."

In my native place in India, we hardly have any specialized palliative homes or long-term care facilities. The only option is to go to the emergency department of the hospital. At 1:00 a.m., the duty doctor came and looked for signs and symptoms, determining morphine shots were what was needed. I consoled my grandma with a smile, reassuring her that she would be alright once they gave her pain-relieving medication. She asked, "Is this medication going to take my pain forever?" Her pain began to subside around 3:00 a.m., and she was finally able to sleep.

When disease in the body attacks our peace of mind, we may fall back to a place of being uncomfortable, and perhaps depression will set in. We may struggle to fight to bring our minds back to a normal, depression-free state. I believe active listening and holding hands in such a situation work magically to bring the person back to a sense of hope and positivity.

Initially, my grandma accepted the disease, but when the pain began, she became depressed. We were able to bring her back to a lesser state of depression by holding her hands and offering reassurance so that she felt cared for and loved.

Day by day, her body weakened, and help with daily life activities was required. She was content to some extent that at least she was not fully bedridden. Six months later, it was astonishing to see her energetic, as if she came back to a life without any disease. However, we continued observing drastic weight loss and loss of appetite.

A steady decline is unpredictable with ups and downs. While on an up, we may think that something good has happened with the disease, the person may seem jovial. At times I felt my grandma was okay and more like her old self, active and doing things on her own, even singing again. And some days, it seemed as if she would pass that day.

The day she told me she had some wishes to accomplish before she left the world, I began wondering what she could possibly mean. She whispered to me, "I need to sell the inherited property of mine for my funeral ceremony expenses." I replied that we would make the arrangements for that while reassuring her that I would not leave her. Her second wish was to go on a long journey. It was after a long period, my grandma agreed to a journey even with her declining health. To achieve that goal, we carefully transported her to our car. She really needed to be transported by ambulance, but that was not her preference. I was obeying her wishes. She was firm that she did not want an ambulance when she was still alive in front of the house. With the counsel of one of my friends, a doctor specializing in homeopathy, she helped us. My grandma was very happy to sit in the reclined front seat, looking at the pristine beauty of nature. I noticed it gave her a sort of relaxation. Later she told me, "I was flying!" The doctor was waiting for her on our arrival and jokingly asked my grandma, "Who told you that you have a disease? You are alright." I still remember the smile on my grandma's face when she heard this.

Motivational words bring positive hope. I once heard that seeing a doctor in and of itself may reduce the anxiety of a diseased person. Similar to the placebo effect. In most cases, we're stressed out about a visit to a doctor; however, for my grandma, when we went to the hospital to see the doctor or even just speaking over the phone with the doctor, she felt better because someone (a medical practitioner) was acknowledging her pain and addressing her fears and concerns.

The doctor read all the reports, observed her well, and gave two medications in liquid form. Afterward, we went for a short trip along the beachside, a road she loved. We reached home safely, and Grandma shared how much she loved the trip and asked me, "Does this medication bring any change in my condition?" I held her hands, saying, "Sure." I thought she needed positive reassurance.

To our surprise, it worked. She never complained of pain or needed to go for morphine shots after that. That was a real mystery for us because the medicine had worked for her, but this may not be the case for another person, as the doctor explained later. I strongly believe the doctor's influence with positive encouragement helped her activate a natural cure in her body.

As those golden 365 days passed, cancer couldn't wait to start ravaging her peaceful memories and exchange them with powerful delusions and memory loss soon on its way. I actively tended to her and went through her world of delusions, reorienting her slowly by first reassuring her. One day she ordered, "Bring a stone to keep this bedlinen to stay firm here!"

I wondered at first, trying to interpret what she was saying. I tried correcting her, "Are you kidding?" I asked. But later, I realized it might have been part of what she was going through. I comforted her by telling her that we could keep the stone over it, even though there was no stone. She replied, "Yes," and soon went into a deep sleep.

A few days later, she was booked to see a neurologist and received tranquilizers which calmed her mind and sedated her. The medicines were specifically colored, and so she used to say, "I will take red one at night," and I didn't hesitate to provide the medication. We were really thoughtful of ways by which we could support Grandma with non-medication by sitting beside her for long times, talking, holding hands, arranging visits with her friends, taking her outside of her room, reading the Bible loudly for her at bedtime, and in the day-time giving her the Bible with bigger bold fonts so she could read even with her vision as reduced as it was.

She preferred to listen to devotional music, sing along with a smile, and pray. Sometimes she would say, "I haven't had any food." She couldn't remember that she'd had a meal only a few hours before. We offered her food whenever she asked. When it happened the first time, we thought it was important to make her understand that she had had all the meals. I came to realize that end-of-life caregiving is about prioritizing the needs to be addressed for the person for their wishes even if it didn't seem the right thing to us.

Behavioral changes are unpredictable, but they seem to follow a pattern with mostly repetitive talking, screaming, yelling at a person caring for them, and crying alternating with laughing. At times the caregiver may think they themselves need counseling. It's true that the family could benefit from counseling rather than the person at the center of care.

When my grandma was nearing her end, her condition shifted to delirium, making up stories from memory, accusing others of moving things, and not caring for the caregiver/s. While my grandma's caregivers were doing their best, she accused them of things and yelled at them for groundless things. Often, a few days after an upsetting event, she would seem to return to a more normal mindset. At first, I tried convincing her we were indeed caring for her. I couldn't understand that this delirium and dementia had to do with her condition. Our family decided to go for counseling for our own anxiety and concerns. My grandma would always eventually seem to come around and be more like her old self. We learned not to argue with her because that would trigger additional outrage. There was no point. Counselling supported our family because it gave tools and language, and ideas on how to cope with these outbursts.

We were happy to see our grandma rejoicing on her eighty-fourth birthday. She had survived one year when it was expected that she would only live for six months. Nine more months passed with a pronounced decrease in daily life activities and becoming bedridden. I massaged her with pain-relieving medications, assisted in taking her to the washroom and with eating. I was disappointed when she began taking food in only small portions. It is hard to see when a family member is not eating well and becoming dehydrated, putting added pressure and stress on loved ones who care so much for them. To worsen the situation, she started dropping down while trying to walk on her own with the aid of a walker. One day she fell before anyone could assist. I was so sorry for her, but with God's grace, she didn't acquire a bad injury. She laughed and kept smiling, saying, "I am a baby now." My grandma never wanted to use an incontinence pad and insisted on using the washroom; after the fall, we took extra care with each washroom trip to avoid falls.

Meantime I received employment for a project at a cancer center, but it was a long way from my hometown. Consequently, my dad and mom, both having chronic ailments, had to support her during those times. I returned on weekends to provide respite care.

My mode of transportation was by motor bike. One day it was heavily raining. I kissed and hugged Grandma in the morning; she blessed me, keeping hands on me, and I rode to my workplace. There were many waterlogged areas on the road, and God helped me to drive through them. It was a tiring day for me, and I became very stressed. For relaxation, I watched the world outside through a windowpane of the cancer center.

Looking at nature with relaxing breath, meditation, and listening to music relieves a lot of stress while we are on a challenging path of caregiving. Even looking out a windowpane can bring relief.

On one particular day, a patient in the hospital for chemotherapy jumped out of the building. I was stunned, and my mind filled with that day's stressful moments. I reached home around 8 p.m., tired and ready to sleep, when the phone rang with a call from my mother saying that Grandma was serious and to please come home. The urgency and despair in her voice prompted me to start home immediately, and by God's grace, I reached home safely in the early morning.

As I look back, I think the added stress of that day helped prepare me to handle what would come—big suffering. When I reached home, I saw Grandma perfectly good with more energy. I was astonished, but later I understood that it was the last big flicker of her candle, which was about to burn in full.

Her vitals were normal, and medication was offered; she took the medication and asked if she really needed to take the capsule and "Do really this capsule can save me now?" She took the pill, and we saw her fingers and feet start widening, her bent knee became straight, and her body released a bowel movement. In a matter of a few seconds, she turned her head to one side, her eyes half-closed. We wondered if she was leaving us forever. We wondered where she went. There was a time of silence. It took time to understand that Grandma has passed away. Sadness came to us like a wave. We all wept and hugged each other, informed relatives and the church. The obituary news was given to the newspaper agency.

Death is inevitable, but it leaves scars on the minds of loved ones. However, we may be thinking our grandma had lived these many years, and it won't be a big issue in our mind, but it was a big deal because I loved her so much, and I really didn't want to lose her. She was my motivator, my spiritual counselor, my everything. Through school, she was encouraging me through my studies and exams. In everything, she provided unconditional support and love, and I felt too much pressure in my chest, which I couldn't open to anyone—vulnerability. I had to sort through it on my own.

She had died in 2009. She taught me first to deal with things spiritually. I thought of going to a church at first. I stayed there for two days, taking a room. The church was near the sea, and there was a cool breeze from the sea. I shared my pain with the sea, spiritually, and through counseling with a priest. I engaged in my own healing, and I felt that someone was consoling me—like a cool breeze—consoling my mind and my soul. Every time the cool sea breeze came, it was as if my grandma had her hand on my neck comforting me, telling me everything would be okay.

While I was grieving, a few things came to my mind, especially about the last few days before her death. One night Grandma told me, "Listen, did you hear the sounds of black crow?" I responded that I did, but truly I didn't hear anything. She told me that it's the "call to bring the boat to take me on time." On the day before her death, she told me, "My boat has arrived." To console her, I told her, "I'm not sending you for the boat brought by a bird," but who can resist the call once called up in God's time? So that was a sign that she was giving us that she would be going soon to Eternity. She had once told me, "When I die, it won't take much time, and I don't want to be bedridden in a coma state." She left us just as she had told me she would. Approaching her death, she used to sing a few lyrics of one particular devotional song, "Who will help us when we are called back, neither friends nor relatives and who can say I can't go back."

In India, we don't have funeral homes. It's the family's responsibility to take over funeral arrangements. A family nurse came to clean her body, which was then taken to a nearby hospital for embalming and then adorned in a white dress. Meanwhile, at home, her bed was arranged by family members with white linen on it. Church authorities brought two big candles placed on either side of the bed and a Holy Cross positioned in the middle. Candles would stay lit until the ceremonies at home were finished. All of the loved ones came, hugged each other, and shared in their grief. Prayers and singing were ongoing, and because all her relatives were living nearby in town, we didn't need to keep the body for a long time. Once we had arranged for the coffin to be delivered to the hospital, we received Grandmas' body from the hospital by ambulance back to the house for public visits. People from far and nearby started coming; some offered a wreath, some presented a small white cloth to put on top of the body as is the custom. We were consoled by people who gathered; it helped us with our grief.

In the old days, the body would have been taken to the church in a decorated wheeled cart pulled by family members. But that is not in practice anymore. We arranged for an ambulance to take the body to the church, and I accompanied it inside. A mobile choir sang devotional songs, leading the ambulance. Family members accompanied behind the ambulance, moving in a slow procession.

Once we entered the church, the coffin was carried by intimate family members only, and only men. We entered the church through the back door carrying her coffin and slowly moving to the front. The coffin was placed in the middle, and close family members sat at two sides of the coffin. Almost an hour-long funeral included ceremonial practices and prayers. Later on, there was a speech about my grandma by church members, and a family member addressed everyone, thanking them for assembling at the church. The relatives and friends offered final kisses. And then finally another hard part, leaving our loved one's body.

When we were all sitting beside the coffin, we still felt our loved one with us. Once the body was taken from the church, many of us cried a bit loudly. The coffin lid closed, the body was carried by family members to the graveyard for burial. The climate was pleasant. And with the coffin set aside near the grave, the priest began the final ceremonial prayers. Just before the burial, the coffin was opened, and the family members put handfuls of sand inside the coffin, and her face was covered with a white cloth. The coffin was closed for burial and slowly placed inside the grave. With our hearts broken, we all said goodbye to meet her on that beautiful shore of Eternity. A small gathering with refreshments was held outside the church after the official part of the funeral was over. And then we were left to go home without Grandma. Anymore.

That void left when we lose our loved ones is a very hard thing to cope with, especially when they lived in the world for such a long time seeing many generations. Our belief is that we are very lucky if we can see our future generations—sons and daughters and their sons and daughters—and even if we see that for more than three generations, that is very lucky. But someone who has experienced that, their age, we miss them. They have been an integral part of our lives. Nobody can replace their position in our lives because everyone is unique. Even if we say we do not remember them every day, they are still in our hearts. We cannot delete their impact on us.

It was a *questioning day* for me. Why did she leave us soon? How can I be happy without her? The empty room where she once slept brought tears to my eyes. I realized she was my main source of positivity from my younger age. I would miss her encouraging words and acceptance of life as it takes us without much complaining. Her assets were not wealth but love and innocence. I decided to sleep in my grandma's room, and my memories were full of Grandma and the stories that she had told. In a dream, I saw her coming to meet me. She smiled at me. It took me an hour to realize that she was no more, and then I asked her how she was here. After that dream, my grief reduced as I saw her happy. The journey continues with memories of my grandma. To my surprise, a rose bush planted by her many years before, which had not bloomed for a very long time, began flowering for the first time after her death. I looked at the bright pink flowers, and they reminded me to stay positive even though I missed her. My grandma used to say to pray for her even after death, and so special prayers were offered at church on her Remembrance Day.

We are tagged with our death day on one day, but if we could know the date, we will never be happy dreaming about the date. Everyone who comes into this world has a birth date. It is my belief that everyone has a death date too. We are unaware of our death date, hoping that we will live for a long time, but if we think we would know that we would die early in life, we would not be happy. Therefore, we are not granted the knowledge of the date on which we will die.

This was my first experience with end-of-life care in my life in a home environment. From person to person and family, it differs in how they are planning to care for a person at the end of life. Initially, my decision about my grandma was that she should have the surgery followed by treatments in the hospital. But when I spoke to Grandma, I realized the importance of not ignoring her wishes. For her, she felt security at home with family members in and around her even though when she worsened, it took more time to reach the hospital and get treated for pain. In my hometown, we do not have long-term care homes or hospice care programs. The impact for me is how much I value having long-term palliative care homes. It reminds me of the importance of the role of long-term care residences, palliative care floors in hospitals, and hospice care palliative homes or hospice programs and how they play such an important role in providing a dignified death for the end-of-life journey.

"The best way to find yourself is to lose yourself in the service of others."

~ Mahatma Gandhi

What was taboo

My grandma's wish was to die at home, and I thought I might have to go against her will and call the hospital for emergency help at the end. That isn't what happened; my grandma died peacefully at home as she wished.

Resources I tapped into

- Guidance and help were received through prayer to handle the reality that I was losing my grandma.
- Support from my parents, relatives, and neighbors for giving care to my grandma.
- Spiritual support came from prayers from members of my church.
- My friend, a doctor, directed treatment and helped my grandma to overcome the pain caused by the terminal illness.

A moment of revelation

I learned that when nearing death, especially in a steady or slow decline death, people seem to have an inner feeling that they are leaving the world soon. They talk directly about it, or there are some cues that we consider hallucinations. I learned that there is a time to die, which the dying person might be aware of, as the body signals that there is not much living to do and it's time to die.

Also, my grandma had an inner wish to live even though the doctor said she wouldn't live more than six months. When my grandma learned that she had stage III cancer, she took the bad news with a smile and never displayed any signs of depression. She prayed and miraculously lived for two years, almost completely pain-free. I learned that natural medications and support can help manage pain as they did for my grandma. She avoided morphine and emergency hospital visits after receiving natural support from her naturopath.

I've become more aware and learned to notice. I have had multiple near-death experiences, always with a kind of premonition beforehand and an inner feeling that something terrible was about to happen. Then I would experience a sense of a driving force after the accident, and I would see helping hands or a way to come back to life.

Self-care tips that helped me

On my first death experience with my grandma, I felt as if I was very heavy, and I felt unrelaxed. Physically I seemed to be jovial, but my heart was pounding with pressure. I decided to get spiritual healing. A week after her death, I went for a long trip driving alone to a church located near a beach. I stayed there for a lengthy meditation, expressing my grief as only a few tears. I felt synchronized with sounds of sea tides and sounds of birds which I could listen to in the peaceful environment inside the church. The cool breeze coming in between touched me physically as if someone was trying to console me. Slowly I recovered from the immense stress to a more regulated, normal feeling.

<u>For the physical body</u>
- Walk in the early morning.
- Maintain a relaxing environment by setting a suitable room temperature and turning off bright lights.

- Regularly make your bed smooth and wrinkle-free, sleeping no more than six hours a day.
- Clean up the room often.
- Enjoy light music, preferably using headphones.
- Enjoy a hot shower.
- Experience small outings on weekends to parks or other places of tourist attractions.
- Hydrate your body with lots of water and healthy nourishment (avoiding heavy dinners at night and consider a fruitarian diet).
- Seek fun times with family and friends.

Self-care tips for caregivers

Maintaining a caring and supportive work environment, offer help for co-workers in need. Be a good listener and motivate with positive assurance while a caregiver is under stress.

I remember a co-worker who ran to me crying and looking for some consolation as a resident who they were caring for was at his final moments. I didn't know the resident, and I was busy with my work, but we ran to reach out to his hands, holding them and praying. I saw the nurse much more relaxed than before. Later I asked her why she was so upset when the resident was dying because usually, she would attend many end-of-life moments. She replied, "He asked me to be with him while he was leaving the world," and she wanted to keep that promise even in her busy schedule and with the stress and overwhelm she was experiencing at the time.

Tips for practitioners

I wish someone would have initially counseled my family and me about the stages we may go through while caring for my grandma. For example, I didn't know about the hallucinations and delirium a person may experience during end of life and how a caregiver can address them, especially while caring for the person at home.

The impact on me about this experience

I entered into the caregiver role. My understanding of caring for a person at the end of life became a blessing, bringing meaning and life purpose for what I am called to do. The experience reinforced my belief that there is eternal life after death and strengthened me spiritually.

What I wish I had known when I began on this journey as a practitioner in end-of-life care and what I discovered about it

When I was in my twenties, I was not that much concerned about end-of-life care. Once I visited one of my friends at a nearby specialized cancer care center, he took me to the general ward of the center where I saw similar faces like me, my parents, my friends, and small children—all awaiting their end of life. Seeing them drastically changed my perspective on life. Before the door of this ward had opened for me, I never realized how painful it would be for a person at the end of their life to die alone, with no one beside them. It was then I accepted the call to be an end-of-life caregiver.

I wish I had known more about the cues or statements that a person at end of life says as they are making a connection with the final days of life.

℘ ℘

How is the end-of-life practitioner a bold spirit?

End-of-life practitioners are compassionate caregivers. In addition to the suffering of the person dying, they take on the stress and emotion that the family is experiencing. Many families don't have time to look after their loved ones to the extent they wish they could because of their job or, in some cases, because of their own illness. The end-of-life practitioner is stepping in to care for their loved one in their absence. Also, the dying client may have questions and concerns that they either have not asked their family or their family or others refuse to answer. And although the end-of-life practitioner may not be able to address all of their questions fully, the practitioner still does whatever they can to offer reassurance.

How is the informal caregiver a bold spirit?

The informal (family or friend) caregiver tries to do for their loved one whatever they can. I have been in situations where the family caregiver was ill, even awaiting surgery for themselves but still wanting to care for their dying parent. And although they could not care for the parent to the extent they wish they could, they helped the best they could by taking on some of the tasks. And even if they are not well themselves, they do their best to step up and help in whatever way they can, even if they are sick or unwell. They are a bold spirit because they are really engaged. They learn whatever tasks and activities are necessary to care for their loved ones and push through those they've never done before. They get involved in managing the caregiving schedule, even if they can't do the tasks. They play an important part of making sure their loved one is cared for.

How is the person who is dying a bold spirit?

It is my belief they have a feeling that they are leaving the world. For some, they keep on trying with their own routines by themselves, at least to some point. For example, they often try using the spoon at mealtime, even if just a little bit. I've often seen them maintain a mentality of keeping themselves strong in the time of dying. They want to be independent as long as possible, even at the last moment. And that takes boldness.

What makes you a bold spirit in end-of-life care?

When I think of myself, I think of one particular client who lives sixty kilometers from my home. He needed care early in the morning, 9:00 a.m., until late at night, 9:00 pm. It's a long journey for me to get to that client, and I'm often returning on the highway, from that remote rural home, in the dark. I return home and feel alone, my young family often already asleep. I take all that risk—driving in the dark on the highway—for someone else and their family. And I don't have to remind myself to have a smile on my face because I know the importance of what I am doing in helping someone else. I miss my family, but I'm focused on the critical role I have in caring for this person and their family.

What's the boldest thing you've done as an end-of-life practitioner?

I have met some elders, in their mid-to-late-nineties, who were extremely physically weak. Every morning, in the long-term care residence, we take temperatures of our residents, and some personal support workers (PSWs) are very afraid to enter a room when they see a resident not moving. In my experience, some PSWs would run out of the room frightened. But I didn't and don't run out. I face the situation. And I saw eight people in two weeks die. In two weeks, those eight people died, and I was with them. Five of those eight people were dying at the same time. I was there with them. Not all PSWs could do that out of fear or whatever was going on for them and stepped away. I did not fear death, and I stood with them to the end. Even when they were given CPR, I was with them, holding their hands. To their last breath—their death.

As an end-of-life practitioner, I want . . .

. . . encouragement and support.

Some days, for example, if you take on multiple caregiving shifts and include traveling long distances, as practitioners, we can feel physically weak and emotionally exhausted. That's the time we need something to boost us. We need some kind of encouragement or support. We also need respect for our work because it deserves to be acknowledged as important as any other job in the healthcare system.

෴ ෴

Siby Mathew Varghese , PSW

Siby was born in India and immigrated to Canada in 2019. He uses his knowledge and research skills from his Master's in Zoology to bring his passion for science to caring for people. Siby has worked on Bio-research projects in the Health sector, completed his Personal Support Worker training in Long Term Care and Retirement Residence, and currently works in Home Health Care. He lives in Toronto with his wife and baby girl. Siby believes God called him to become a compassionate caregiver.

Contact information:

+1 647-575-7935
sibymv@gmail.com
https://www.linkedin.com/in/siby-mathew-varghese-639435195

Book Recommended by Siby Matthew Varghese

Integrating a Palliative Approach — Essentials for Personal Support Workers
by Katherine Murray (2014)

This book absolutely inspired me. Each of the chapters gave me insights into how to be a good caregiver, and I was particularly interested in the section that helped me to truly differentiate between how empathy and sympathy differ and how empathy can help me more meaningful while we care for a person.

About the Book

"This book was written specifically for personal support workers, healthcare assistants, nurse's aides, etc. It will engage you with its warmth and heart, and provide you with the necessary resources and tools to respond to the needs of the dying and their families. Filled with practical strategies, stories of caregiving, and real-life scenarios, Integrating a Palliative Approach will increase your confidence and competence in providing compassionate care for the dying. In reading this book, you will learn the importance of - Integrating a palliative approach into the care of people with any life-threatening disease, early in the disease process, across all care settings - Reflection and maintaining therapeutic boundaries - Communication, and how to avoid roadblocks and open the doors to conversation You will also learn about - Common symptoms, and tools to help you gather information and provide comfort measures - Psychosocial needs, and how to create a nurturing place and respond in difficult situations - Last days and hours, and strategies to use in caring for the dying person and family - Self-care and compassion fatigue, and ways to care for yourself - The health care team, and strategies for advocating and communicating." ~ Amazon

CHAPTER 6

USING MY VOICE

"My life has been a quest for knowledge and understanding, and I am nowhere near having achieved that. And it doesn't bother me in the least. I will die without having come up with the answers to many things in life."

~ Alex Trebek

The hospice chaplain whistled the entire time we bathed my mom, and I tried to tune her whistling out. My main focus was making Mom comfortable, even though she was unconscious. Mom loved Andrea Bocelli, one of her favorite songs was "Time to Say Goodbye," sung in a duet with Sarah Brightman.[51] Dad brought his portable tape player and played the song repeatedly as we all sat around her bed. She was on oxygen, and the noisy, big bulky machine was at her right side, where Dad sat next to her. We watched as Mom's breathing became slower and shallower, waiting for her to transition.[52] Dad turned off the tape player, removed her oxygen, and we watched her take a few sips of air, and then she was still. I looked at the clock on the wall; she left us at 2:28 p.m. Moments after she took her last breath, there was a gentle, cool breeze that floated around each one of us, and a sense of calm and peace filled the room. No one was crying anymore. We all sat there, trying to make sense of what we were feeling.[53] I believe this was one last gift from Mom; that gentle, peaceful, loving breeze was her soul, touching each of us, her last physical way of telling us that she was at peace and that we would be too.

I had imagined this moment in time for months, not knowing what to expect or how it would look and feel when Mom passed. I had been grieving her loss months before it happened. We had a special bond. I was her firstborn, and she was there to watch me take my first breath. I was there to witness her last. The journey that led up to this moment in time was eight years long, chaotic at times, laughable, gut-wrenching, and even joyful. Mom was born on Mother's Day, and she transitioned on Mother's Day, seventy-six years later.

---

[51] Needs of the Dying #14
[52] Needs of the Dying #12
[53] Needs of the Dying #15

My path to being her medical advocate on this journey started in March 2000 when I was diagnosed with stage four, papillary thyroid cancer. For eight years, I had asked every doctor I saw to explain the lump and my symptoms. Those who felt it would order blood work and tell me my thyroid levels were fine and I just needed to stop eating so much and lose weight. No one ever explained what a thyroid was or how it affected the hormones. I blindly accepted their responses until I visited my dermatologist for an unrelated issue. The results were, at age thirty-eight, I had thyroid cancer. At my surgeon's appointment, I was prepared. I had done some research and had a list of questions ready, and I was taking detailed notes. My doctor was concerned I wasn't taking this seriously "because he could read my handwriting."

I looked him in the eye and calmly responded, "You're not with me when I'm alone." At that point, I understood what it was to be my own medical advocate. I had to be the one to educate myself, my parents, spouse and prepare my children for what was coming.

When I was alone was when I could feel the fear and uncertainty and let my emotions show. The surgeon and I were the same age, he had five children and had not had a patient as relatable as me, so my experience helped him understand and treat future patients with a different perspective. This was before patient-centered care was created or adopted by doctors, nurses, or hospitals.

It is critical that you be your own medical advocate. I learned the hard way to ask questions, and if I didn't get a satisfactory response, I got a second opinion. Or a third! I wouldn't take what any doctor told me at face value. I learned if I didn't feel comfortable with the information I was given, to keep digging, keep asking questions, and not be placated.

    This lesson is what made me the medical advocate and caregiver I am today. On May 12, 2003, my mom's sixty-eighth birthday, she woke up with a large lump behind her left ear. We went to see her general practitioner that morning. Within a week, a biopsy and results were shared. She had non-Hodgkin's lymphoma. She started treatment with one oncologist but wasn't comfortable with her care and aggressive treatment options. She got a second opinion from a different cancer hospital doctor and felt more comfortable with a new oncologist. At every appointment, I took detailed notes, asking the doctor to spell words and define them so we all understood. Sometimes we would bring a tape recorder and record the discussion. Some doctors requested we not record the appointments. In several cases, those doctors were replaced. Something I noticed right away was that when doctors knew I was Mom's medical advocate, they would start talking to me instead of looking at and talking to her during appointments. I would politely stop them and say they needed to speak directly to Mom.[54] When some would continue to speak to me, I would look down at my notes and not make eye contact. It's so important that doctors and medical staff engage with their patients directly; after all, they are the ones living with the diagnosis, and it's very important to build a trusting relationship between patient, doctor, and caregiver.

    Patients and caregivers (usually family) have the right to be treated with dignity, compassion, and respect, to have time to ask questions, to decide for themselves what procedures they will or will not allow medical professionals to administer, to receive a copy of all doctors notes from every appointment before leaving the

---

[54] Needs of the Dying #5

office, to receive copies of all reports from MRIs, CAT scans, X-rays, bloodwork, biopsy results, and any other documentation without having to pay out of pocket for it at a later time. Always be sure to ask for copies of any test results you've had done and the doctor's notes from that appointment before you walk out the door! You are legally entitled to these documents, and it makes being educated and organized much easier moving forward. Many hospitals have adopted an online patient chart access system. As a caregiver, you can create this patient account for your loved one with their permission. In this way, you have more options to set up appointments, email the doctor, retrieve test results and doctors' notes, etc. Caregivers who care for elderly family members can take advantage of this electronic system and save everyone time and frustration.

We learned this the hard way when Mom changed from one cancer hospital system to another for her treatment. She was told she needed to provide all her doctor's visit notes, tests, and treatment records to the new hospital facility. She called the medical records department to request copies of all her records from the last three years. It took over a week to gather copies of everything, cost several hundred dollars, and we had to use a suitcase with wheels to carry everything home.

During the early stages of Mom's cancer journey, she had been accepted into a clinical trial. As her caregiver and medical advocate, I kept detailed notes of her reaction to the treatments and, as part of treatment, learned how to give her intramuscular injections as close to the original vaccine site so she didn't have to go back to the hospital for the next three days to complete the trial treatment.

Lymphatic drainage massage was one more daily routine that was added to her growing list. Mom was not happy that she was not told before having the lymph node removed to create the custom vaccine that she could develop lymphedema as a side effect. Another word of caution, be sure before agreeing to any procedures or clinical trials that you have a thorough discussion of what side effects could occur if the procedure is done. This also goes for any type of treatment. Mom did not go into remission for five years. After all chemotherapy options were exhausted, Mom had a radio-active isotope treatment and went into remission for almost two years. We were not told before accepting treatment that one of the side effects was the development of acute myeloid leukemia (AML), which is what took her life.

Being a caregiver to Mom was a labor of love, one that I would do again in a heartbeat. Was it difficult at times? Yes! The days where she had multiple doctor appointments were hard on us both. I made it my mission to be her voice, her caregiver, and her daughter. The days I was with her, I was not with my children and spouse. By the end of those days, I was mentally, physically, and emotionally drained. I knew I was neglecting my family, but my parents did not have any other support, and as the oldest child, I felt obligated to take care of them. I was a "sandwich generation mom," my family understood why I was not there to take care of them. But knowing such things logically cannot always make up for feelings of guilt and neglect. I would carve out time for my family, doing things individually with my children and spouse as often as I could. We made it through, my children are grown and witnessed by my example, how to lovingly work through tough times and appreciate the good in life. We continue to share a strong, loving bond.

I have younger siblings. Two live locally, and one is out of state. The siblings who live locally decided that they could not be supportive or watch our mom's health decline. They did not want to take any responsibility or help her and Dad, instead deciding to remove themselves from the situation. Family dynamics during times of crisis is a situation I am all too familiar with. At first, we were all shocked at my siblings' decision. Mom, Dad, and I really needed their help. Even if they couldn't bring Mom to a doctor's appointment, they could have come to visit, brought the grandchildren, sent cards or notes, made a phone call, helped with household chores, cooked a meal—something, anything would have been a big help. Their abandonment shook my parents to the core and left me with total responsibility for Mom and Dad's care.

In the beginning, I was deeply hurt and angry by my siblings' actions. I tried talking with them, pleaded with them to help, but my pleas fell on deaf ears. I didn't have time to dwell on their abandonment. My only option was to do everything possible to support our parents. Because of their abandonment, I did suffer from physical, mental, and emotional exhaustion.

After Mom passed, it took a full year for me to recover physically. I have since forgiven them for their actions, I have tried to rekindle our relationships, but we are still estranged. I will always love them, but I do not trust them and don't know if I ever will. Keeping the grandchildren from Mom was the worst part. Mom cried over this for the last two years of her life. When she was in the nursing home, and our parish priest came to give her last rites, the first thing she said to him was that her children were still keeping her grandchildren from her. Father Sal told her that didn't matter right now. Right now, she needed to focus on herself and the transitional journey she was soon going to embark on. I knew this was weighing heavily on her heart, and I felt helpless to help her feel better.

My siblings did have the opportunity to speak with her before she died. What was said between them, only they know. Within a few days, Mom was in a coma. She did not wake up.

Mom has been gone for ten years now. Our family has not reconciled. Dad is still crushed by their actions. I know how much Mom cried in my arms over their actions. I'm sure she cried in his arms as well. We live a "new normal" life with missing family members. To cope, I live by the Serenity Prayer: "God, grant me the serenity to accept the things I cannot change, courage to change the things I can, and wisdom to know the difference."

Caregiving during COVID-19 has presented many new challenges. Now, even more, family support is required, but I have spoken with non-family member caregivers who are still not being supported. Many long-term care institutions were not accepting new patients or residents, which left families scrambling to create and implement care plans in homes and apartments. When there are few or no family members to help with daily basic needs care, these elderly individuals are left alone to fend for themselves. The rates of elder abuse and neglect are rising to alarming levels.

Even without COVID-19, there are fewer viable options available. Independent companies that provide companionship, non-medical support services, and visiting nurses can be hired privately by family caregivers. Sadly, it often comes down to cost. Many seniors do not have long-term care insurance, and often families cannot afford to pay out of pocket. Those who do have insurance or private pay do not necessarily have the option of providing the same person upon each visit to care for loved ones. Trust issues and stress for seniors are avoidable when the same caregiver is assigned to provide care. There is also the risk of sending in a caregiver who may be asymptomatic. This can lead to distress for everyone. Currently, there is no one size fits all answer. This situation continues to be a work in progress.

We thought we had time to talk about and make final arrangements before mom passed. She had all of the legal paperwork completed: will, living will, and power of attorney for medical and durable. The one important conversation we did not have was her final wishes. There never seemed to be a good time to bring this up, especially when we were coping with her cancer treatments. Where did she want to die? Did she want a traditional church funeral, to be cremated, to be buried or—?

When Mom was in the hospital and the oncologist told us there was nothing more they could do for her medically, we were devastated. After a few hours, the oncologist pulled me aside and told me I had one day to make plans to move Mom from the hospital. I was not prepared for this. The hospital social worker came in to explain what our options were and made referral suggestions. Instead of spending precious time with Mom, my youngest brother came into town, and he, Dad, and I were out visiting nursing homes, meeting with the church staff to plan her funeral, visiting and making final arrangements with the funeral home, picking out her casket, and purchasing her cemetery plot.[55]

Because we never discussed it, I found out too late that Mom wanted to die at home. I had already promised her that I would take care of Dad when she was gone. I worried that if she

---

[55] Needs of the Dying #16

died at home, he wouldn't be able to live there anymore or that he would become despondent and depressed. I felt terribly guilty about not fulfilling her last wish. I now know there are so many options available for all of these final wish arrangements. The final wishes conversation is not an easy one to have or think about, but I've lived the alternative. So much chaos, stress, cost, and heartache could have been avoided, if only, and I'll say it again IF ONLY we'd had an open, loving, and honest conversation before we got to this last part of Mom's life!

I firmly believe directive planning is a vital part of being an adult. Once the plans are made, this guide or road map is one of the most loving things you can do for your family. The nice thing too, it can always be changed depending on life event changes. I urge you, for your peace of mind and your family's, to have the conversation. There are many wonderful online resources available that can help you with checklists and the best way to start the conversation.

The local hospice we worked with is one of the largest and most well-known in Northeast Ohio. After Mom passed, I was contacted by the hospice supervisor. We talked about Dad. I was concerned for his mental and emotional well-being and asked if there was grief support for us through their facility. I was told that only one of us was allowed to participate in their grief support group for a limited number of visits. I made sure Dad signed up and attended the meetings. I, on the other hand, had to figure out how to work through my grief solo. The first couple of years, I was emotionally numb. I couldn't look at a picture of Mom, think about her, or even talk about her without bursting into tears. As time went on, I coped, lived day to day, sometimes moment by moment. Life events would pop up, my parents' anniversary, Mom's birthday,

Mother's Day, all grim reminders of her not being here. It took me over five years to be comfortable with remembering Mom, looking at pictures again, and talking about her with family and friends without crying. I still have moments where I wish I could call her and share an event that occurred or just tell her I love her.

The grieving process is different for everyone. There are now more labels for grief and bereavement than ever before. As a woman who has lived her life doing most everything on my own, I didn't know where else to turn outside of family and friends for grief support. Thankfully things are different now. More support groups and grief counselors are available to help those who need extra support work through their loss. Even with these new grief counseling sources available, please know it's okay to work through your grief at your own pace. No one has the right to tell you when you are done grieving, ever!

This is my story of how and why I decided to become a certified end-of-life doula. I was already doing the work before I even knew this support existed professionally.

If the last twenty years have taught me anything, it's that even though we will all leave this mortal coil, we as humans are finding our way back to nature. We are being reminded that to live well, we also have the gift of dying well. The hospitals, nursing homes, and funeral industry have taken the personal touch of death and limited remains disposal options. It's institutionalized, compartmentalized, and has removed many generations from understanding, embracing, and facing the fear associated with death. We fear what we don't understand or can't explain. It's a natural response and personal choice how we deal with it. I am happy to say that due to the death positive movement, remain disposal options are expanding slowly throughout the United States.

I am truly grateful that I was a participant and witness to my mom's cancer journey. As her caregiver, I had the instinct to protect her at all costs. I lived with the guilt I felt for not making things better for her, the relentless drive I had to do whatever it took, some of my actions may have caused my siblings and family to feel shut out. It certainly wasn't intentional. My parents were private people, and at times, Mom didn't trust anyone outside the family; often, she only wanted my help. Several experiences with doctors and healthcare staff left her afraid to speak up when she wasn't comfortable with her care. Speak Up programs are now encouraged and promoted by healthcare institutions and providers.

I have learned that there are other resources available, so caregivers have time to focus on self-care. Self-care is not selfish but a necessary part of the process. In addition to new avenues of support available, I find by practicing acceptance and letting go of guilt makes me a better advocate and caregiver. There are agencies for the aged to find local resources for caregivers, money, and benefits available through Medicare, Medicaid, Veterans Benefits, long-term care insurance, and other local options to provide services and caregiver respite. My parents raised me to persevere through challenging times.

Perseverance is essential. My own cancer journey taught me how to be an effective medical advocate. As a daughter and mom, I learned early how to be the best caregiver I could be. As a witness to the chaos and stress of not having final wishes and arrangements for my mom before she passed, I developed strong advocacy skills for opening up the final wishes discussion and directive plan preparation. As a human being, I understand logically what grief is and just how devastating it can feel.

There are as many ways to grieve as there are stars in the sky. Now more than ever, the death forward movement is bringing to light that everyone has options and support available to them. Empathy in one's heart and the ability to provide to those who need it, safe, sacred space to process their own end of life journey are essential. End-of-life doulas are the bridge between healthcare, hospice, patients, and loved ones. Each specializes in various areas of the final life journey. My specialties include directive planning, legacy projects, caregiver respite, and bereavement support.

Even though many will resonate with my experiences and journey, there are many more who have not had these life experiences. Mom taught me how to live courageously while dying. For everyone who has read my story, my wish is that you be proactive instead of reactive when it comes to end-of-life decisions. Life is about making choices, and dying is too.

"Everything that has a beginning has an ending.
Make your peace with that and all will be well."
~ Jack Kornfield

---

೮೦ ೦೩

What was taboo

Several years before Mom died, two of my three siblings decided to step away from interacting with Mom, Dad, and me. Our family dynamics at that time were completely fractured. My two siblings decided they could not be part of or watch mom's health decline. After I went to them, pleading for help and getting nowhere, I had to back off and focus on what I needed to do to support my parents.

Talking to my parents about my siblings' abandonment was primarily a taboo subject. Mom was devastated because my siblings kept their children away from her – she was the grandma who lived for and loved her grandchildren! They were her light, and it was devastating to watch helplessly from the sidelines as it was for her to live without them in her life.

Here we are ten years later, and speaking with or about my siblings and grandchildren (who are now grown adults) with Dad is still not something I can openly discuss, and I doubt we ever will.

Resources I tapped into

Working with hospice the last week of Mom's life was a saving grace for me. They came in when I called them at 2 a.m. Mom's leukemia caused sudden, severe spikes in temperature, and the nursing home staff were not responding to my calls for help. The hospice supervisor herself came with a kit for me to help with Mom's comfort/palliative care.

The hospice chaplain came in and helped me bathe mom before and after she was in her coma state; then, after she transitioned, she again helped me bathe and dress her before going to the funeral home. During this time, I had my brother take Dad out of the room for a break. When he came back in to sit with her, he was in awe, exclaiming, "My God, she's beautiful!" Without the hospice volunteers' help and support, this moment would not have happened.

Moment of revelation

While sitting vigil with mom, a hospice volunteer, Eric, was with us. He monitored Mom's progression and, after two days, told us to be ready because the end was near. His presence and support were very comforting. I don't think Mom's passing would have been as peaceful without him.

I do believe Mom gave us one final gift just after she transitioned. As we were sitting around her, we watched her take a few sips of air then go still. We were all crying up to that point. Just after she stopped breathing, the cool breeze that went around each of us, I believe it was Mom's spirit giving us a final hug, her gift to let us know she was ok and we would be too.

Self-care tips that helped me

I have to be transparent here. While I was a caregiver to Mom and support for Dad, I raised two school-aged children. Self-care during those eight years was not a regular part of my life. There were expectations from everyone that it was my responsibility to care for and support my parents while also raising my family. This is commonly referred to as being a "sandwich generation mom." There were days I felt like a stretched doll, being pulled in different directions to support whomever needed it while my basic human needs often went unmet. And I wasn't alone. At the time, I met several other family caregivers struggling with being the sole person responsible for their loved one's daily care. At that point, I didn't know where to find help, and as the person who other's leaned on, I just soldiered through.

Days ran together, and my calendar was my bible. If something happened to that, I was doomed. At this point, too, I was working part-time as a substitute teacher. It was one more way to keep tabs on what my children were doing in school and keep me in the workforce. Yes, I was an overachiever, even though in my mind I felt that I wasn't doing enough to keep it all together, others on the outside looking in couldn't understand why I was so driven, much less how I was doing it.

Looking back now, I know I had a very warped sense of what my "duties" were. My youngest brother was very concerned for my physical and mental well-being, but he lived out of state and could only offer his verbal support. I have learned that self-care is not selfish. Currently, I am the primary medical advocate and caregiver to my elderly aunt and dad. I no longer feel guilty for taking "me time." I eat healthy meals, get six to eight hours of sleep, go for walks and treat myself with the compassion, kindness, and love that I so freely shared with others. I highly recommend self-care practices; after all, you deserve to live your life even in the service of others.

Self-care tips

Be sure to listen to your body. Get enough sleep, eat healthy meals, make time to shower, and take a walk or meditate to clear your head. When caring for a parent or loved one and raising children, be sure to make time for your family. One-on-one time with your children is time you won't get back. I understand trying to juggle caregiving and parenting can be extremely difficult, especially if you are a single parent. Try to find a friend who can help you stay grounded and pitch in when schedules become overwhelming.

Self-care tip or strategy for caregivers

Do your research. When caregiving for a family member, research their condition to effectively communicate with healthcare providers and hospital or hospice staff. The more you know and understand, the better the care and the easier it will be to make sound decisions moving forward.

Tips for practitioners

Self-care is not selfish. It's the best way for you to help someone else. When you are physically, mentally, emotionally, or spiritually depleted, you cannot provide the best possible service to others.

Help start the end-of-life conversation with loved ones. I understand how difficult this discussion can be, but the alternative is much harder for those left behind. When your loved ones have no guidelines from you about how you want to die, where you want to die, what medical interventions you do or don't want, funeral plans, and so forth, they are the ones who will struggle and scramble to fulfill those responsibilities. We plan for birth, be responsible, make those decisions now while there is no crisis, and plan for your death. These plans are not written in stone, and they can always be amended as new life events occur.

The impact on me from this experience

This whole experience started twenty years ago with my own health crisis. I learned that it was vital to be my own or have a medical advocate. When I became a caregiver to Mom, I quickly learned that hospitals, medical staff, and support staff all have their own protocols, and they frequently do not communicate or interact with each other. There is little consistency in how each group conducts business. Everything I learned throughout the caregiving process has led me to become a certified end-of-life doula.

I am no longer afraid to speak up or to have difficult end-of-life conversations. I firmly believe the best way to live life is to have my final wishes prepared and shared with my loved ones. Without having these plans and discussions in place, I would be neglecting my responsibilities and placing an unnecessary burden on those I love. I won't do to them what was and is still being done to me.

What I wish I had known when I began on this journey as a practitioner in end-of-life care and what I discovered about it

For me, end-of-life care is as natural as breathing. I have been doing the work for family and friends most of my life. I am honored and blessed to have the love, compassion, and patience in my heart to do this important work. I have the opportunity to continue to learn new methods in care and help educate and support those individuals and families before the transition journey begins or work with those whose transition journey is progressing.

I now know that dying and death are not to be feared; they are a natural part of life. I wish I had had the strength and courage to include my children more in the process when Mom, their grandma, was actively dying. I know they are both afraid of dying and death. A conversation my mom had with my fourteen-year-old daughter still haunts her. Neither knew how to address this conversation, and I didn't find out it even occurred until a few years after Mom passed. My children were not with us in the nursing home when Mom died. They didn't get to witness her final gift to us, and even though I've shared the experience with them, it's not the same. They weren't there to witness and feel what transpired in that room, to see the peaceful transition, or to really say goodbye. I feel I've done a disservice to my children for not including them in this experience.

I am trying to help them through their fear of dying and death by having open discussions with them. I have also started to share my final wishes with them. I will not do to them what I experienced with mom. It's a process getting them on board, they are still uncomfortable, but with planning and love, I will continue to keep our communication honest and open.

ಸಿ ಇ

Why can we call end-of-life practitioners bold spirits?

Practitioners are bold spirits because they have unlimited love in their hearts to help those who are either in transition or preparing for transition in an honest, holistic way. They are warriors and advocates. They want to make sure that the person they're supporting has a smooth transition and can let go of any earthly worries, family disagreements, or anything else that is hindering their peace. That's one of the big things that they are advocates of—to help people die with peace and dignity.

I believe that when you are caring for a loved one, the practitioner is their warrior and often the main advocate. Until an individual walks the path of a proactive medical advocate, they may not know how to effectively communicate with healthcare practitioners, doctors, or hospital systems. Each has protocols that are often different or inconsistent. In navigating each pathway, sometimes through trial and error, can one find the best care. Sometimes one has to step in and advocate for changes because the doctor or healthcare facility did not do what was best for the patient or provide the best care. Often, the end-of-life practitioner must do whatever it takes to help facilitate changes in care and should not feel apologetic for where their heart is. Caregiving and advocating for someone is a labor of love, a calling, and a gift for those giving and those receiving.

Why are informal caregivers bold spirits?

Every step of an end-of-life journey for an informal caregiver can be like a trial by fire. They usually volunteer to walk that path with love, curiosity, confusion, and fear. They walk that path with their loved one to help them along the way so that they don't have to continue to suffer alone from whatever it is that they're experiencing. Not being formally trained, the person taking care of a family member in a medical or end-of-life situation often struggles to determine how and what the best course of action is. And sometimes, they fall short, while at other times, they exceed expectations. No matter how each challenge is met, informal caregivers are needed, appreciated, and are definitely bold spirits.

Why is the dying person a bold spirit?

To be actively dying and to still function on a day-to-day basis is such a roller coaster ride. There are going to be good days and bad days. Depending on that person's fortitude, perseverance, the way they view life, and the fears they may face or overcome regarding their impending death, they all contribute to them being a bold spirit. They are walking a journey that they have never consciously traveled before.

If the dying person is not functioning actively in daily activities, can they still be considered a bold spirit?

They are still a bold spirit, as long as they're drawing breath. Sometimes people have a strong will to live because they have unfinished business with someone. Even if they are bed-bound, they can think, speak, and interact in other ways. For example, they may communicate with eye movements or sounds. They can still connect with those who are around them. The person who no longer draws a breath, the person who dies, is still a bold spirit, just on a different plane. They have transitioned from their earthly body and moved on to another realm. That bold spirit does not die. It's just that we don't see it on this earth anymore.

How is it possible to consider a person who is dying a bold spirit when they choose to "give up" when they decide to take a final breath? Is that possible in your mind to still consider them a bold spirit if they choose not to fight and not stay alive?

Oh, absolutely. That's their choice. And nobody gets to judge what another person decides because they are the only ones living in their physical body and experiencing their physical existence. Living and dying is a physical, mental, emotional, and spiritual process. So for someone to be ready to let go—for example, due to terminal illness—their physical body begins the process of shutting down until they stop breathing. It is not something that you can put a label or time limit on. It is not something that anyone else but that individual can decide. By making that decision to fight or by letting go, that is a bold choice. That is being a bold spirit.

As an end-of-life practitioner, what makes you a bold spirit?

I am able to separate emotions from the process. Instead of making the person that I'm working with suffer needlessly, or not understand something, or not be educated in certain areas of their process, I'm able to step back and assess the situation, which helps me be effective and make their and their loved ones' journey more peaceful and calm. That's one of the big things I am happy and grateful to do for others. Sometimes it is more challenging than other times to separate emotions. It is called compartmentalizing, and I can set aside my personal feelings to logically focus on the actual problem or challenge at hand. It doesn't mean that I don't cry about it later. Having clarity and being level-headed, being a little bit less emotionally attached, makes a big difference in providing guidance and support. This whole process is not easy for anyone.

In your role as an end-of-life practitioner, what is the one boldest thing you've done?

The boldest thing I have done as an end-of-life practitioner is learn how to use my voice and speak up. When being an advocate for someone, speaking up is important. And I've had a personal struggle with speaking up for a long time. I'm at a point now in my life where I do not hesitate to speak up. When I see something, I say something. I make sure that I approach it in a non-confrontational way so that the situation gets resolved. The boldest thing I've done is learn how to use my voice and speak up.

What is the second boldest thing you've done?

The second boldest thing I've done is learn how to be present while someone is actively dying. I've learned how to embrace, not shrink away or look away from someone actively dying. I open my heart, acknowledge, accept, and holistically support everyone experiencing this end-of-life journey.

As an end-of-life practitioner, I want . . .

. . . to help educate people not to avoid or shrink away from this experience.

I want to help others be more present, take a more active role, do directive planning, make final wishes known to loved ones, have open, loving end-of-life conversations, and take the steps necessary so that a mess isn't left behind for loved ones. This is because I've lived what happens when someone who has died hasn't done what I've mentioned. As an end-of-life practitioner, my goal is to help those individuals and their families open their hearts and minds, embrace the challenges to be faced, and openly communicate to make the experience easier for themselves and the person who is actively dying. When someone can be fully present and make decisions to be proactive instead of reactive, the dying process can be a peaceful and beautiful experience for everyone.

ഈ ൚

Janice Lombardo, CEOLD

Janice has over twenty years of experience as a medical advocate, caregiver, and cancer survivor. She has and continues to lovingly provide physical, psychological, and psychosocial holistic support to those in transition and their loved ones. She became a certified end-of-life doula in April 2020.

Since 2007 Janice has provided both patient and caregiver perspectives to help improve hospital systems and protocols for relationship-based and patient-centered care as a volunteer on the Patient and Family Partnership Council, Acute Care, Cleveland Medical Center, University Hospital's main campus, in Cleveland, Ohio. She is a member of INELDA, the International End of Life Doula Association. Janice is a certified SAGECare (Senior Action in a Gay Environment) advocate, offering her end-of-life doula guidance and support to the LGBT community, seniors, and their loved ones. A teacher at heart, Janice looks forward to keeping abreast of new end-of-life options and sharing them with future clients.

Contact information:

www.MyAngelJaniceCEOLD.com
email@MyAngelJaniceCEOLD.com
MyAngelJaniceCEOLD@gmail.com
(440) 494-6263
Facebook: MyAngelJaniceCEOLD
Wickliffe, Ohio 44092 USA

Book Recommended by Janice Lombardo

Accompanying the Dying: Practical Heart-Centered Wisdom for End-of-Life Doulas and Health Care Advocates
by Deanna Cochran (2019)

This book was relatable to my own caregiving experiences. The end-of-life journey is very personal; there is no right or wrong way to face your mortality. Family members are often thrust into caregiving completely unprepared. Having relatable resources to guide and glean information from was priceless. This book helped me more fully understand and appreciate what goes into being an end-of-life doula. The author shares her experiences and insights into how the calling to do this work is rare, and that compelled me to look at my own calling to this work. I came to better grasp the idea that there is fear for many people in this sacred transition, and I want to be part of relieving that. The author made it clear that it's not the caregiver's responsibility to make decisions for people who are ill but to provide options available and suggestions of people or institutions that can help.

About the Book

"Accompanying the Dying describes the human skill and art of companioning someone through dying. There is a wide gap in this knowing (of how to accompany the dying), which is why this book is timely and needed at this juncture of the "death positive" movement. The book is meant to empower us as a society to understand how to die well in this modern age. Deanna describes the newly emerging role of the "end-of-life doula," which is a nonmedical role that provides practical, emotional, and spiritual support to the dying and their family. This role is a powerful solution to the looming crisis in health care as our baby boomers and their elders age and die in the oncoming years." ~ Amazon

CHAPTER 7

BULLSHIT! YES, I CRY

"To those who fail to live forever: may something here find its use in your coming days.

~ Stephen Jenkinson,
Die Wise – A Manifesto for Sanity & Soul

We sat in her living room, Brenda in darling pajamas and a pearl necklace. She had been an ample woman and was relishing being able to fit into cute little clothes, and so we had brought bags of size *cute* for her to try on from our local ladies' clothing store. It was so much fun watching her try on pieces that she had never before been able to wear.[56] She embraced the fun. From the day Brenda was told she was sick, she had begun wearing a string of beautiful pearls. The pearls were something she loved but realized she never wore. She wanted to be buried wearing them, and in a cute little outfit, with her hair perfectly coiffed . . . no "undertaker hair" for Brenda.

We had been friends for about four years and enjoyed a mutual friend group that had fun around bonfires. We laughed until we cried, threw amazing birthday parties, and were secure enough in our friendships to be able to talk about *anything*.

I had just accepted the position as director of our local volunteer hospice organization when Brenda was diagnosed with cancer. I clearly remember the day our friend group was all together, and she told us the frightening news about her health. She stared at me and said, "You and I will have a discussion at a later date, if and when the time is right." This broke any discomfort between us. It was like we had signs on our foreheads: mine read "I am hospice," and hers read "I have cancer."

At the age of forty-five, diagnosed with stage four esophageal cancer, Brenda was aggressively treated with chemotherapy and radiation and then had her stomach removed. The time came when her oncologist told her and her husband Joe to contact hospice. In a small town, that meant me. Now I would become her hospice caregiver—my role as hospice director also included direct patient support—and it was time to talk about how she wanted to move forward.

---

[56] Needs of the Dying #1

As a practitioner, this made me sad and nervous at the same time. This was my first experience caring for someone I knew so well. But, I found that the sadness and nerves helped me dig deep.

I had only been doing this for a very short period of time, and I didn't have any training; I was going in with my heart and instinct. For resources to focus on what I knew to be true: the care of an actively dying person is not complicated. It requires calm focus to support not only the dying person but those around them. I proceeded to do my job as a hospice caregiver practitioner and be there for my friend and her husband. Truthfully, having them as my friends made the process of moving forward intimate and quite lovely. We had a connection that included humor and sometimes inappropriate giggling when we became tired, or something struck us as extra funny. I realized I was being invited on the last journey they would take together. And it was a privilege.

Upon Brenda's admission to hospice, she decided that she wanted several things to happen.[57] First, a renewal of their wedding vows was important to Brenda and Joe. An event in their backyard, it would include delicious food, the obligatory bonfire, and people dressed in their most colorful clothing. It would be a testimony to their marriage and commitment to each other as they moved forward through the journey ahead. There was not a dry eye when we listened to their vows, nor a dry eye from laughter as stories were shared long into the night.

Second, in conversation about her ultimate transition, Brenda made it very clear that she had no faith. She did not believe in God. Brenda believed you were born, and you died, and that was

---

[57] Needs of the Dying #2

it; there was no life after death. She was adamant that neither she nor Joe would require any spiritual support.[58] She knew she wanted to die at home under the care of her husband and those of us that could help support her. This conversation was a bit tough for me, as I absolutely believe in a higher power and a peaceful place after death. It is important as a practitioner, however, to follow the lead of the patient. I have learned from supporting more than seventy-five families that death for me is hopeful, and I am not afraid. I needed to support *Brenda's* beliefs without imposing my own. Only privately could I pray for her peaceful journey.

Third, Brenda wanted to dip her toes into the Pacific Ocean one more time. I panicked when I thought of the logistics of this extended trip. It meant that there needed to be medication support for her along the way, not carrying too many controlled substances. It was also important to ensure that she would have medical support if her condition worsened along the way.[59] Medication access through hospices and hospitals along the route was arranged, and she carried her medical files and prescriptions and felt comfortable going forward with the planned trip. Joe rented an RV, and off they went! They had a seamless trip, and she dipped her toes into the Pacific Ocean, feeling quite accomplished. The trip went off without a hitch.

About ten days after they came home from the RV trip, Brenda called and explained, "Now is my time to let go. Can you come?" We live in a very cold part of the country, and when I received the phone call that night, the weather was miserable. It was November, and a storm had started. I packed a bag and headed to their home. Nancy, a strong and supportive friend, their best

---

[58] Needs of the Dying #4
[59] Needs of the Dying #10

friend, was there when I arrived. Nancy and I had not always seen eye to eye, but she was a gift during the death vigil, and my respect for her helpful compassion blossomed and remains solid to this day.

Because Brenda had had her stomach removed, she had a port for hyperalimentation, liquid nutrition, and her only source of nourishment. At her request, it was disconnected. The next primary focus was to make sure Brenda's pain was under control.[60] Pain patches and dissolvable under tongue medications were the most reliable. These allow the medications to quickly enter the bloodstream. Comfort next, even though they had set up an adjustable bed in their guest bedroom, Brenda insisted she wanted to be in her king-size bed and sleep next to her husband.[61] With heaps of pillows and blankets, we made that possible. The larger bed provided easy access for friends and family wanting to lie with, hold, and comfort her. Joe and Brenda had an active intimate life, and their bedroom held many memories of love. She sat like the diva she was, wearing her pearls. It felt right. At one point, Joe asked me what to do with the toys in the bedside drawer. We giggled like teenagers and decided they should be put in a plain paper bag and disposed of.[62]

During our first evening together during Brenda's final days, the storm that had started on my way over became an ice storm. Roads were closed, as was the airport. Brenda's family lived far away, and the assigned hospice nursing staff could not get out to the house, and so I became the sole hospice caregiver for her. The ice storm lasted for three days. I was grateful for the medication and swabs we had stocked at the house and the fact that

---

[60] Needs of the Dying #10
[61] Needs of the Dying #5
[62] Needs of the Dying #14

I was a nurse. We had food, heat, and each other. When one of us became tired and needed to rest, another took over.

One couple close to Brenda and Joe made the journey through the ice storm to visit and say goodbye.[63] Brenda wanted to sit up at the bedside to visit with her friends, so we arranged it. We set up chairs close by for her friends. I lay in behind Brenda to support her with pillows. When the friends arrived, they asked what they should do or say. "Just be you!" I encouraged and set a timer for twenty minutes, all that Brenda could tolerate for a visit. I also suggested that, if they were comfortable, to let her know they would make sure that Joe would be well taken care of after she was gone and that it was okay for her to let go.

They had a pleasant visit, lots of talk about the awful weather outside and some fun stories of times spent together. When the time for their visit reached the end, Jennifer, through tears, looked at her dying friend and said, "We love you and want you to know we will take good care of Joe. Honey, it's okay to let go." Without missing a beat, Brenda calmly looked down at her friend and replied, "You go first!" We all completely lost it! We laughed so hard, Brenda almost fell off the bed. Sometimes humor wins.

There comes a time when the dying person is physically present in the room but starts to fade into a different dimension. This is "the grey area," which most people refer to as transition. It's when those present in the room become less of a focus of importance to the dying person, and they move into a space that seems to be in between here and gone.

---

[63] Needs of the Dying #1

This is the toughest time for loved ones, as they feel their role in the dying person's life has changed and become less significant. It is often a clear event where the physical presence is taken over by spiritual presence. After witnessing this so many times, it appears to be a protective phase, possibly making it easier for them prior to their final letting go.

I remember Joe saying he couldn't watch his wife as she entered this new phase. "She doesn't see me anymore," he wept. To help Joe find comfort for him as she continued her transition, I suggested that he sit in behind her and hold her, he did, and we added extra support with pillows. And boy, oh boy, did she transition. When Brenda headed into the grey of her journey, she started to talk. And she talked, and she talked, and she talked— for about thirty hours straight.

Brenda talked about how long the bridge was on several occasions. I have heard people say this before, more often than I hear them talk about white light. She introduced her husband to someone. "Please" and "thank you" were often repeated, and Brenda called out numbers—three, four, twenty-nine—almost like she was calling out bingo numbers. She'd bellow, "I'm stuck. The chair is in front of the door!" And much to our surprise, "I'll pray for you." Finally, "I'm in here with my cancer."[64]

She was not talking to any of us physically present in the room. She was having very clear conversations with people that had died. She would look at different locations in the room and chat with whomever she saw there. Joe's brother had died many years prior as a young man, and she was greeting him by name; they were discussing how to decorate a room. Occasionally she would look at

---
[64] Needs of the Dying #4

us and say, "I've never decorated a room like this before." Her father and grandfather were part of her conversations, too. She said to someone, "You don't need those pin-ups anymore; you're too old!" and then laughed. Like in life and good health, Brenda kept her sense of humor until the end.

Just as Joe felt helpless when Brenda floated into the grey, so did Nancy and me. We were really only able to bear witness to her conversations and felt in awe of how intensely present others were to her, even though we could not see them.

As Brenda's chatting settled down, she started asking for her mother.[65] Brenda's mother lived thousands of miles away, so a phone was in order. She was encouraged to tell family stories, tell her daughter how she felt about her, and sing songs from her childhood. Placing the telephone on the pillow next to her head, we left her alone with her mother, checking in on her periodically.[66] Because Brenda was already in the grey area, between here and gone, she was unaware that her mom was not physically present in the room. Joe said when he got the phone bill that the call had been three-and-a-half hours. The phone bill was not important. The comfort and the calming that it brought to them both were immeasurable. After the call ended, Brenda's incessant chatting almost completely stopped.

Overhearing Brenda's mother talking and singing and being with her daughter was emotional. I shed tears during that time, reflecting on how it would feel if that were my daughter or my mother. I had had a similar situation when my father lay dying years later, he in Canada and me in Mexico. I had asked the nurse

---

[65] Needs of the Dying #15
[66] Needs of the Dying #6

to put the phone on his pillow so I could speak with him. I also sang to him for about a half-hour. It brought me so much peace to have had that connection. The nurse told me he cried and smiled all at once. He died a few hours after our phone conversation.

On the morning of what would be Brenda's last day, Joe was standing at the foot of the bed, and I was lying next to her when she said, "I need you to pray with me."[67] Joe looked at me and expressed an expletive. Under normal conditions, I would have called our chaplain to come to pray; however, we were still in the midst of an ice storm, and a visit was not possible.

It happened that a good friend had faxed through that day's devotional, and it was spot on for the moment. That is what I read to her, followed by the Lord's Prayer. I kept it simple, and she seemed even calmer. I was a bit dumbfounded but deeply grateful she had come to this place of requesting a prayer. In my opinion, a spiritual focus undeniably helps bring the brain and heart to a peaceful place; it helped me achieve a sense of peace, too, after so many days awake.

After two days of terrible weather that also impacted air travel, Brenda's sister arrived. Knowing that Brenda could feel her presence, Sue sat with her, holding her hand and reading one of their favorite childhood books. Brenda was a non-spiritual person. And around their house, they had all sorts of cartoons and furniture like from the well-known story *Alice in Wonderland*. Brenda was peaceful and at rest. Sue believes that Brenda waited for her to arrive before leaving earth about twelve hours later.

---

[67] Needs of the Dying #9

Brenda died peacefully, her husband lying next to her. It was November 29, 2015, at 4:30 am. Joe mentioned that Brenda's arm had moved to touch him as he watched her take her last breath.[68] We sat with her quiet body in peaceful silence and shed tears of sadness and relief that her difficult journey was over.

A sense of relief after someone dies is very real. Often the intense journey family and friends have endured leaves them feeling relief and, as such, a big sigh of relief. And with that, guilt sometimes creeps in. To cope with this feeling of guilt, I often compassionately offer that they have gifted their "person" by caring for them at home, in their own environment, until their final breath and that there is no greater gift you can give to someone. They have done everything they could, and there should be no guilt about that.[69]

After Brenda died, it wasn't long before the formal caregiver role in me kicked back in. Under normal circumstances, the deceased's assigned nurse would come to pronounce the death and bathe the body. But road conditions prevented that person from attending. Families used to do this for each other as a caring last act of kindness. Nancy and I agreed to do it together. It was Nancy's final gift to her best friend.[70] [71]

Our local grocery store owner, and friend, generously plowed the driveway so that the funeral home director could come and transport Brenda's body. We packed her last suitcase, including her *new size cute* outfit, polka dot bra, red lipstick, hair gel for when I would give her that perfect coiffed hair, and her forever pearls.

---

[68] Needs of the Dying #15
[69] Needs of the Dying #1
[70] Needs of the Dying #16
[71] Needs of the Dying #16

And then . . . like she had calmly said to her friend about who was going first, she went first.

 ⊱ ⊰

What was taboo

Taboo was putting my beliefs into Brenda's journey. She was clear about not having faith in God or a higher power. You live, you die, and it's all done, was her belief. My belief system is very deep in how I operate daily in the world and very different from hers. I had to tuck my beliefs onto a shelf to help me, help her. And not to impose.

Resources I tapped into

I was new to the field of hospice and had no formal hospice training. I did, however, have a background as a registered nurse and had worked extensively with people in psychiatry and people in pain. I mustered internal confidence, as I have throughout my life. Lesson learned from my persistently optimistic mother!

Moment of revelation

My aha moment was realizing that telling people "It's okay to let go" can have interesting results; you never know what the patient will say. In Brenda's case, her humor came shining through as she said, " You go first!" I have used the statement "It is okay to let go" often and never had someone say, "No, I won't go." More often, they seem to relax into the permission.

Self-care tips that helped me

I need to stay hydrated and fed when spending a long time with a family. I don't recall what we ate, but we realized that both were necessary to keep up our strength to care. It was odd that sleep didn't seem essential over three days. I think that adrenaline took over.

Self-care tip for caregivers

When I was seeing multiple clients a day, I would take about five minutes in my car prior to moving to the next home. I would center myself with a prayer of peace and then physically do a "cleanse" of myself, using a gentle cutting action with my hands in front of my body to separate the experience that I had left and cleanse me for encountering the new one to come.

Tips for practitioners

Listen to and watch your patient. You will learn so much about moving through this process. Remember that dying is something we do. It doesn't happen to us. Witnessing what people do is how we learn.

The impact on me from this experience

Remember to believe in my ability to care for people who mean a lot to me. I was so concerned about caring for a friend, and it had been more comfortable walking into the home of a stranger and caring for them and their family. In the end, the privilege I felt in being able to be so close to my friend while she died was a gift of immeasurable depth.

What I wish I had known when I began on this journey as a practitioner in end-of-life care and what I discovered about it

I wish I had known that as people let go of their worldly bodies, it is really like laboring through birth to get into the world. There is a lot of internal work, and the external world is not that important. There is a separation that happens before death, as when Joe found it hard to see how Brenda didn't see him anymore.

℘ ☙

Why are end-of-life practitioners bold spirits?

End-of-life practitioners tread where others fear to tread. That's what gives practitioners some boldness. And I think it's sometimes unexplainable to others that end-of-life practitioners are willing to go where others won't.

Why are caregivers, those who are not paid, bold spirits?

They are bold spirits because of love. They might think they can't, but because they care so deeply about someone, they do. It's similar to the commitment I've seen in marriages, where the family/friend caregiver says, "I said till death do us part, and I have kept every vow I took. And this is the last one." Often I see that family caregivers say they don't know what they're doing, but they're willing to do anything they can manage to support their person who is dying.

What makes the dying person a bold spirit?

The boldness comes from making choices they can be comfortable with as they face their death. They don't have a choice that they're dying. The boldness comes from a decision in how they want it to go. It's bold to move forward with those decisions because some people you talk to indicate that they want to pull the blanket up over their head and just let it happen, which is a decision. And that's a bold decision too. But deciding to live as much as they can until they die is also bold. They're all bold decisions when you're told you're dying.

What makes you a bold spirit as an end-of-life practitioner?

Meeting you. Honestly, you have been the biggest kick in the bum for me. I can't believe I pressed play that day to say, "Yes, I'm interested in your book," because it has changed my whole winter. And that's made me bold! I have stepped out of a comfort zone. I'm going to get out there and butt heads with, for example, my local hospice because I'm going to take my decades of experience and be the new option. I feel like I've gained confidence and boldness in the experience of writing about my experience with end-of-life and hospice work, and knowing that I know what I'm doing, I'm moving forward to become more public and vocal.

What is the boldest thing you've done related to end-of-life work?

The boldest thing I've done in end-of-life work is learning to drive a boat at night to get to people in need during end-of-life transition. I had to put aside my fear, put aside my anxiety to go be with people. Driving on this lake at night is terrifying, but I put people before myself, which isn't very smart sometimes. I think it's bold to sit at the bedside as people are dying and to have everybody around you, putting aside one's own emotion. You don't want to cry, and yet bullshit—I cry!

As an end-of-life practitioner, I want . . .

. . . to educate the broader community.

I want to help people manage the fact that they're afraid of death. I love doing that piece of it, going in and talking about it. That educational piece is important. Helping people complete their end-of-life planning is important. I've learned to be really comfortable in sitting with people to address it. Through COVID, I've also been helping many of my friends, peers, and colleagues complete their end-of-life paperwork. It's important to do it and then let it be. You don't have to constantly think about it.

I think people will be calmer about facing their end of life if they're informed. And when people are calmer about end of life, that can bring about an easier time for their loved ones, an easier time for them when it does come time to their death.

I was in Mexico for Dia de Los Muertos, the Day of the Dead's celebration, and I sat for hours and wrote the names of every person that I had helped with their dying experience on a little wooden fob that you would get at a craft store.

We had a huge altar at my aunt's house. I came in with four loaves of bread with sixty-six names of the dead and placed them onto the altar. The Mexican people just about fell over because normally they have grandma, grandpa, whoever's died within their family, but I came walking in with these four loaves and all these names. And to them, those are all spirits.

They were freaked out, baffled that one person carried so many spirits with them. When the bells started chiming at 3:00 pm, gong-gonging in this tiny little village of Teotitlan del Valle, in Oaxaca, the wind whipped down the valley and slammed the doors of the altar room shut. And they looked at me and went, "See? See the impact of all those spirits? Thankfully, I was there with an aunt who spoke English, but the rest of the people present were all local people.

That was pretty bold of me to do that. It freaked them out for two days. It was so cathartic for me to have all those spirits walk with me that weekend through the village and do their thing. It was awesome. You talk, you eat, you drink, you tell stories, you cry. Uncle Arnulfo used to say, "It goes in as Mezcal," the local alcohol, "and it comes out as tears." And it's so cathartic. Once a year you get to celebrate everybody. Here in our society, we tend to want to hush about it, "Oh, poor Grandma died. We don't want to upset anybody by talking about her." And I think that is part of education too. Celebrate our people.

Gale Gagnier (formerly Reynolds McKie)

Gale is a registered nurse (graduate of Toronto Western Hospital). She has had a wide-spanning career in psychiatry, industrial health, and a founding partner in a consulting company called BodyLogic Health Management. This company offered injury prevention and pain management programming to industries around the world. Her strength and passion for public speaking made her a sought-after presenter in health and safety management.

Upon her retirement from consulting work, she became the director of Koochiching County Volunteer Hospice. It is her focus and passion today, and she offers private practice death support within her community under her business name Final Wishes. Gale is a certified death doula and an active member of NEDA (National End of Life Doula Alliance). Gale continues to speak on death and dying and the role of death doula and hospice support at her local community college and in community forums. She offers an interactive lecture, What It Is Like to Die, that is well received and has quite an impact on participants. Gale is also a family mediation practitioner in her community.

Gale lives full-time on an island on Rainy Lake with her husband, Mark. When she began doing hospice work, she had to learn to navigate their boat in the dark and severe windy and wet weather to respond to client's calls for need in the middle of the night.

Contact Gale Gagnier:

PO Box 134, International Falls, MN 56649
galegagnier1@gmail.com
218.324.0226

Book Recommended by Gale Gagnier

The Five People You Meet in Heaven
by Mitch Albom (2006)

The author opens the book, "It might seem strange to start a story with an ending. But all endings are also beginnings. We just don't know it at the time." I feel this way each time I meet a new family and enter into their journey.

Eddie, the main character, teaches each person he meets a lesson: the power of lost love, sacrifice, forgiveness, letting go, and acceptance. At the end of the book, the author writes, "It is because the human spirit knows, deep down, that all lives intersect. That death doesn't just take someone, it misses someone else, and in the small distance between being taken and being missed, lives are changed." "Time," the Captain said, "is not what you think." He sat down next to Eddie. "Dying? Not the end of everything. We think it is only the beginning." What a hopeful thing!! Thank you, Mitch Albom.

About the Book

"Eddie is a wounded war veteran, an old man who has lived, in his mind, an uninspired life. His job is fixing rides at a seaside amusement park. On his 83rd birthday, a tragic accident kills him, as he tries to save a little girl from a falling cart. He awakes in the afterlife, where he learns that heaven is not a destination. It's a place where your life is explained to you by five people, some of whom you knew, others who may have been strangers. One by one, from childhood to soldier to old age, Eddie's five people revisit their connections to him on earth, illuminating the mysteries of his 'meaningless' life, and revealing the haunting secret behind the eternal question: 'Why was I here?'" ~ Amazon

CHAPTER 8

WHAT'S UP WITH DEATH ANXIETY?

"The way we regard death is critical to the way we experience life. When your fear of death changes, the way you live your life changes."

~ Ram Dass

One question I've come to ask myself is, When does the end-of-life process start? When I was a kid, this was very interesting to me as I would notice if someone in the community was dying, and my instinct was to be involved in some way. I asked a lot of questions to my parents' dismay because they were not sure how to approach the topic.

When our first pet died, I started to distrust the end-of-life process thinking of it more as a failure and something to be hidden. Our family cat died tragically in an accident that left my parents reeling. They were grieving themselves, and they weren't sure how to break the news to their toddler daughter. So, they didn't. It was a lovely story that they told me, which involved the kitten having started a new life somewhere else. But I knew they were not telling me the whole story and wondered why.

As I was growing up and trying to make sense of the world, I often thought of my first pet. Where was she now? Would I ever get to see her again? These questions were ones that would transform in my mind over time. Eventually, I would start to think of myself as that being, the soul that lived inside of my cat. At around the age of eight, I knew what had happened to this being. And I felt like I had missed out on an experience of grieving that loss.

Some nights I would think about an accident happening to me. Would my story be the same as my tiny kitten's? Would those whom I loved and who cared for me sweep my death under the rug? Would they lie about what happened and not allow others to grieve my passing? It all became so upsetting to me that my curiosity gave way to fear, disdain, and obsession with death, dying, loss, and grief.

When I was around the age of thirteen, I attended a funeral for the first time. It was for one of my childhood friends' mother, who died of lung cancer. I felt sad for the family and sad that we would no longer see our friend's mom in physical form, but at the same time, I was so comforted by a proper memorial service. This was proof that deaths were treated with respect and that there was space to grieve the lives lost and share the beautiful memories we all have with them.

When a grandfather I had never met before died and I learned I could not attend his funeral (it was a flight away and I had school), I was upset. I felt as if I was being shut out from grieving again and that I did not seem important because I did not know him. I explained that I wanted to know him, and I was grieving that loss tremendously.

All these experiences curated a perfect storm for the anxiety I would experience about death and dying as a high schooler. I was a naturally anxious kid, especially about death, but it became so all-consuming that it felt as if I could not concentrate on anything else. I couldn't believe that those around me could live their lives so blindly as it seemed as though they didn't think about death at all.

The only person I related to at all was my mother. She had stress about death and dying, but it was more so worrying about her kids than worrying about herself. This created another layer because while I understood the fear she felt it also made it easier for me to internalize my feelings of fear. I started to have ideas around what it meant to live, a success to me, which meant death was the failure flip side to that.

I'm sure I don't speak only for myself when I say that I wanted to make my mother happy—we all do. It is a unique experience, though, that the meaning of happy means to survive so that another does not experience pain. In this way, I was trying to control my mom's feelings by making sure I didn't do anything that would make her upset, and the big one which would make her the most upset would be my demise.

I know I'm not painting an extremely rosy picture but stay with me because I know this is resonating with some of you, if not all, and we are going to get to some good parts.

When I was in high school, I ended up in the emergency room every other week worried about a different terminal illness. Every time a death would be covered in the media, or it happened around me, I would search for their symptoms, and then I would experience those symptoms and think that I was suffering from the same illness. It seems rather sensational, but I went to great lengths to catch anything early so that I would not die an "unnecessary death."

I was then diagnosed with generalized anxiety disorder (GAD) and health anxiety (or illness anxiety) which provided some relief at the time that I was getting help from counsellors. What I noticed was that there was still a blockage between what I was experiencing and what the counsellors really wanted to talk about.

I want to preface this section by saying that there are lovely counsellors who I'm sure are comfortable talking about death specifically, but those were not the counsellors I was seeing. I also want to make it clear that I didn't specifically talk about my fear as being afraid of death and dying at this time because I wasn't aware of it yet. The taboo was so deeply embedded within me that death and dying were things that I, myself, did not want to think and talk about. This was even when I was obsessed with death and dying. I believe now that this is a big danger with death being taboo and something not talked about in our society, especially for kids.

In my short time so far as a death doula, I have been working with clients around my age and younger. I talk to people every day about death anxiety. I educate the public by holding monthly Zoom meetings (as we are in the era of the COVID-19 pandemic). I talk to parents of kids who are having conversations with their little ones about death. I remember these conversations with my parents, and it is one of my main goals to talk to parents about guiding their child to view death as a natural part of life so that they do not grow up terrified as I did.

What I have come up with to help others like me is the creation of a Death Positive Coaching Program. It's a coaching program that teaches my clients that they can have their own thoughts about death and dying, that they don't necessarily have to go along with what their cultural worldview of this life phase is. Most of those who live in Canada (like me) grow up with death in the shadows where it is not spoken about or shown. The program I created is about reclaiming this space to contemplate death and dying in a healthy way. It's also about realizing that contemplating death is overwhelmingly contemplating life itself.

In the following stories, I will detail some of the experiences I have had with clients in my initial year of working as a death positive coach. All of them came to me with extreme fear of death and dying. And all have another thing in common—they wanted to live life more fully instead of having their lives taken over by intrusive death thoughts. All names have been changed to keep their identity anonymous.

The first client I want to talk about is Caitlin. Caitlin came to me after hearing about me from an online death cafe, which is how most people hear about my work. She had confessed that she had been dealing with extreme fear of death and dying since she was small. There was something about her family's religiosity that did not give her any comfort as a child. With my work being heavily about letting others figure out their own thoughts and feelings while giving them an outside perspective, working with me was an attractive path after the confusion of the religious teachings that made her question her own judgment. There are also children involved in Caitlin's life, which I found most intriguing because of my experience as a child thinking about death and dying. Caitlin wanted to stop the cycle of death denial. She wanted to become more death positive to be able to talk to her kids about death in a more positive manner than her parents had with her. Thinking about what I was like when I was a kid, I wanted to help this mother contemplate her own mortality to allow her kids to explore their own. Once we started working together, it was clear that there were many sore spots with death and dying in Caitlin's childhood. This is typical for those who struggle with death anxiety because when they are trying to figure out their lives, they are having very contradictory information about death and dying. This was the same for Caitlin, and this was the last thing she wanted to pass on to her kids.

One day, I got a message from Caitlin that she had found that their pet fish died. Caitlin was worried about how she would break the news to her little one. All the past experiences from her childhood came back into view, and she worried so deeply that she would make a mistake. My job here was to reassure her to think about what she would want to hear about this death as a child, to think back to what she might have wanted her parents to say to her. A part of it was already finished; the fish was already flushed down the toilet. A memorial with the fish's body would not be an option anymore. We started from where Caitlin was at the moment—with her emotional state. We talked about her thoughts and feelings about the fish's death and having to explain it to her four-year-old.

She did not necessarily want to talk about heaven because she hadn't entirely thought about her beliefs and if she even believed in the telling of creation and the afterlife in the Bible. When she thought about talking about heaven to her kids, she cringed. We explored and thought of something different, something that could be understood in not just this aspect but also in other aspects of life.

Caitlin had talked to me about her thoughts about the process of death being a part of nature, something that happens during the changing of the seasons. I suggested that this was something that might help her little one. It was hard for Caitlin, but she talked about the nature aspect of death and dying, comparing the fish to a flower that eventually dies in nature. The discussion went well, even though it continued later. Caitlin shared that it was a beautiful accomplishment to open up a conversation for the first time in letting her child know that talking about death (and the fish in this situation) is never off the table.

To any parent reading this, it is never too late to have another conversation about death and dying. I realize that it takes your own journey into mortality to allow you to open in a different way with your children and everyone you love, but it is so worth it.

Another client who heard of me from attending a death cafe told me about her intrusive thoughts about death. It almost seemed as if Morgan could not control when and how she thought about death, and it made her think that she was obsessed with death. She decided that she did not want to be that person.

Little did she know ... I was that person! I'm kidding—kind of. I certainly suffered from intrusive thoughts when I was young, and I continue to have intrusive thoughts at times. The difference is that I don't see them as a problem anymore. I interpret them as a window viewing the death thoughts that I want to pay attention to and how they can help me in my life.

Morgan's situation was interesting to me, and I saw myself truly as a support for her as she was already so self-aware and ready to delve in and do the work. It wasn't too soon that she began to see her path and begin to accept herself fully. In Morgan's situation, it was about accepting herself as being someone who thinks deeply about death. For most others that come to me, they see themselves as weird, morbid, or strange. This is partly due to the taboo around death and dying in today's modern world. It has been hidden in the shadows, and every time a young person questions why it is there and tries to shed light on the topic, it is pushed back into the darkness. Morgan had experienced this and had a wound from that experience of being thought of as morbid because of her curiosity.

When working together, Morgan spoke extensively about her thoughts about death itself and her thoughts about her curiosity. We explored what she was feeling in her body when she thought of herself as morbid, and then we took those thoughts and practiced ones that gave more acceptance to who she is. Together, we figured out that there were thoughts that she preferred more and made her feel much better in her body. One of those thoughts was, "I am learning to accept that I think about death sometimes." It took away the hurt and made her feel authentic acceptance for herself and her curiosity about death and dying.

One day in one of our sessions, Morgan remarked, "You know, this is the first time I've just accepted that I'm someone who thinks about death and that it's okay." Her comment surprised me and I ask her to stay on that thought for a few moments because this was a huge deal. Morgan explained that she didn't understand why it was such a big deal. This also didn't surprise me, and I continued, explaining that it's natural after we've reconditioned a programmed thought that we may not realize how hard it was to change. She'd spent thirty years of her life thinking of herself as *weird* because she thought so much about death, and that made her feel anxious that she thought about mortality. In just a few months, Morgan had completely overturned that thought and was now beginning to accept herself as someone who thought about death, and that was okay.

It can be difficult to accept something we think about if it is also something that society does not like to talk about. This pushing away from our own nature to think about our mortality can create anxiety. It is normal and natural to think about mortality, we are human, and we have the mental capacity to think about it.

Another client, Joelene, faced religious trauma in her life. With all my clients, there are often a lot of contributing factors to death anxiety and extreme fear of death and dying, but one of the big ones is belief about the afterlife. There are many ideas about the afterlife from different places and cultures, and one of the insecurities can come from all the different beliefs. We begin to wonder which one is true. This big question came up with Jolene, and I encouraged her to contemplate what she would most want to believe. My personal belief is that the idea of the afterlife is very much for the living. None of us know what it is like to die and to visit beyond the veil (unless you count near-death experiences) so figuring out our thoughts and beliefs is an individual journey. It might be connected to your lineage, but if you don't connect with your family's beliefs, you can explore other beliefs. It's something that I tell my clients is entirely their own journey and that I'm there to be a supportive guide, to ask questions to help them figure out what thoughts are coming up that distract from the work of acceptance of what we really want. Everything that comes up about death applies to life as well.

As I worked with Jolene, it was clear that she was figuring this out for herself. She wanted to believe that one thing happens which would prove the others to be false so that she would know for sure what would happen when she died. Of course, she knew logically that it was impossible to rule out what could happen in the afterlife, which frustrated her to no end. She desperately wanted to know so that she could prepare. The challenge here was that Jolene was trying to find a definitive answer where there was none, causing her spirals by thinking of all the various options and what could happen. This is not something that someone figures out in just a few months.

Jolene had been practicing the tools that I teach by allowing herself to be curious and asking questions about her own beliefs rather than getting caught up in all the options of different types of beliefs. Letting her know that her beliefs were the only ones that matter in her life, giving her a sense of comfort and safety to live a full life that is not consumed by confusion, supported her exploration. One of the thoughts that she began practicing was, "It's possible that I am connected to something bigger." This gave her the sense of comfort to be able to imagine what could be possible and what she would want for herself in whatever afterlife experience exists.

The question of the afterlife is difficult and complex. It is one that many parents, in particular, have a hard time talking about with children because nobody knows exactly what happens. Getting okay with that and finding what works for you is important. Being curious about one's own beliefs in the place of being curious about what other people think about it is essential.

So, how do I help the dying? I have been called to focus my energy on what I am aware of and what I have experienced. I focus on the thoughts or feelings of young people who are contemplating the mortality of themselves and their loved ones. In this way, I am a death doula and a death positive coach who is motivated by changing the culture about death and dying in society in general. I believe the more we focus on the younger generation, the more likely we are to change the culture of death and dying from being taboo to have a society that respects elders and death as a natural part of life.

ೞ ೲ

What was taboo

It's taboo in our society to talk about death and dying in general. By association, it's taboo to talk about our thoughts, feelings, and fears when it comes to death and dying.

Resources that I tapped into

- My psychology degree is a resource I have tapped into and the experience gave me tools in active listening, as well as providing client-centered support.
- Having grown up with death anxiety myself, this experience is something I choose to regard as a resource of mine as well. My experience getting to know my own death awareness and my thoughts and fears about that awareness allowed me to help me support others. I have a ton of empathy for my clients because I have been in a similar headspace.
- And last but not least, my colleagues in this work. Learning from my colleagues has been a huge resource as I am a younger person in this field. I learn from those who have had more experience, and I use their advice to the best of my ability.

Self-care tips that helped me

The self-care that I put into practice myself is compassionate self-reflection. It's not bubble baths and facials all of the time (even though that's also mood boosters at times). For me, it's holding myself accountable to take time to focus on me, myself, and I.

Self-care tip for caregivers

Use a tool like a journal or something else to figure out how to continue contemplating your own death thoughts and death awareness as you are helping others with theirs. This goes much further than just death. Figure out your own thoughts and feelings about life, in general, to relate to yourself while being there for others in your life. It's all about balance.

Tips for practitioners

Start where you are and meet those you help where they are as well. We all have to start somewhere. Above all, be authentic in your work.

The impact of this experience on me

The collective impact of working with all of my clients and learning about how I can support each person with their thoughts, feelings, and fears is that it ultimately allows me to learn more about my own fears as well. I think that the more people share and learn from others, the more open we will be about death in general and all of the thoughts and feelings that come up.

Significant moment

After doing an online course to become a death companion, I found a new friend in a fellow classmate. The most inspiring moment of my death work experience so far was becoming so close to someone else who was just starting out in this work. My friend was most interested in at-home mortuary services, and she inspired me to look into post-mortem support. This friend and I talked about our death-positive life every day and how it made our lives that much better. On October 6th, 2020, I learned that my friend had died a couple of days before tragically and suddenly. I couldn't believe it, and I did not want to believe it at first. I had never grieved a loss so hard in my life, and the one person I wanted to chat with was gone. All of our conversations about how she felt about life and death were comforting because she had such acceptance for her journey. One of the last messages I received from her said that I was doing important work and that she was proud of me. Grief and loss can be a fertilizer for growth and learning, and my friend's death definitely has been that for me, especially since she was so death positive and wants death to no longer be a taboo in our society.

What I wish I had known when I began on this journey as a practitioner in end-of-life care and what I discovered about it

I wish I knew to get into it sooner! I know I am only twenty-four years old, but beginning this journey during COVID-19 has been extremely difficult. I wish I could jump in and become a death doula for dying patients and their families at the end of life, but being in contact with a family poses health concerns during this time. I don't want to put added stress on what is already a difficult time for a family. I wish that when I had started, I would have known how this virus would change things, but at the same time, it is also teaching me to do what I can while keeping everyone safe. This is just one of the many reasons I work remotely and chat with people who experience death anxiety because it is an experience I have worked through myself, and I have the skillset to support others with.

ஓ ଓ

Why are end-of-life practitioners bold spirits?

    Death work in any capacity is activism because it has been such a taboo for the last one hundred years or so. Practitioners are coming into this space of educating people on who they are and what they do while trying to make it a career. Part of it is like taking a leap of faith of knowing that you're going to help many people and hopefully be able to make a career out of it and survive on your own. But part of that is educating people on what you do and how you do it, and what role you have in it. Explaining death and dying doesn't have to be a negative experience. It doesn't have to be hidden.

Why are caregivers bold spirits?

    More likely than not, especially where we are now, there is no respite. There's no time off. The caregiver is in a position similar to a single parent. That's how I view my uncle as a caregiver for my oma, who has dementia. I don't think people make that connection. My uncle supports my oma—feeding her, figuring out which care to have come into the home, or when long-term care will be required. The roles have reversed, and now his mom requires similar care to a child. These caregivers are bold because it takes so much strength and so much commitment. There's more likely than not any time off. And if there is time off, there is that mental toll it takes when not there in person. That *what if?* What if I leave and while in the care of someone else, something happens? Even when there is respite, there's still all of that kind of baggage you take with you.

Why is the person who is actually dying a bold spirit?

The dying are going on an unknown journey. That takes boldness. Think of the analogy of going on a camping trip in the wilderness, and you don't know how it's going to turn out. That's kind of what dying is; it is like going on to the next step, but nobody knows what that'll be like. Death doesn't have to be a failure. Most of our world and most of the Western culture think that death is a failure. Typically the only explanation for death is that you've lived.

What makes you a bold spirit, especially related to end-of-life practitioner work?

I've noticed I'm recently holding back some of my boldness because of some thoughts and opinions that I have that maybe aren't of the majority of death workers in general. And part of my work is working with either teens or young adults and talking to them about their fear of death or their unwanted thoughts about death in general. Teenagers are a demographic where they just think about death more than anybody else.

And so, that is kind of controversial in itself because most of the people that contact me are age sixteen, and I need their parents' permission but are their parents going to want their kid to talk to somebody about death? And there's such a misconception right now that if you talk about death or you acknowledge that you're thinking about death, it's going to make you think about it more. Just in my psychology background, I know that that is not true. And that if you deny that you're thinking about something, that makes it worse.

What makes me bold is that I'm trying to educate on the psychological aspects, and I acknowledge that I'm not a professional in that sense either so I'm just trying to tip-toe on this line of wanting to help people that are younger who are going through this and don't have a role model because at my age when I was sixteen, if someone were to have told me, "Yeah, I think about death too, and it's okay," I would have been like, "Really?" Everybody that comes to me has said they were like this too. I had originally wondered *How does everybody live their lives and think about death as much as I do? Do other people think about death as much as I do and still continue living?* And that's scary.

As a death positive coach, I want . . .

. . . balance.

Balance is the give and take of connecting to my own death awareness and the drive to connect to the way others experience death, grief, and loss. The balance I strike in my work is not easy because I often find myself wanting to focus on others. I feel a lot of death workers, caregivers, and those in supportive care have to decide to focus on the self at times. We are of no use to those we help if we do not think about our own well-being. If I do not check in with my own experience with death anxiety, I will project my ideas and experiences onto my client and diminish a supportive environment. Balance in taking care of oneself and supporting others is key in the work we do as practitioners.

∞ ☙

Ashlee Jansen

Ashlee was born and raised in Nova Scotia, Canada, and she has recently moved back home to connect to loved ones and the death work community. She grew up thinking about the complexities of life, which inevitably brought her to be curious about death. Ashlee supports others with death anxiety after going through her own death acceptance journey.

Contact information:

akinddeathdoula@gmail.com
250-532-3284
www.deathpositiveash.com

Book Recommended by Ashlee Jansen

Staring at the Sun: Overcoming the Terror of Death
by Irvin D. Yalom (2009)

This author talks about how our fears are all connected to one thing—death. It also allowed me to read stories about how the author helped others with their death anxiety which inspired me to do the same, though in different ways.

About the Book

"Written in Irv Yalom's inimitable story-telling style, Staring at the Sun is a profoundly encouraging approach to the universal issue of mortality. In this magisterial opus, capping a lifetime of work and personal experience, Dr. Yalom helps us recognize that the fear of death is at the heart of much of our anxiety. Such recognition is often catalyzed by an "awakening experience"—a dream, or loss (the death of a loved one, divorce, loss of a job or home), illness, trauma, or aging.

Once we confront our own mortality, Dr. Yalom writes, we are inspired to rearrange our priorities, communicate more deeply with those we love, appreciate more keenly the beauty of life, and increase our willingness to take the risks necessary for personal fulfillment." ~ Amazon

CHAPTER 9

UNCHARTED TERRITORY

"**Death is not the opposite of life, but a part of it.**"

~ Haruki Murakami

I was twenty-seven years old when my grandpa was moved into a home for seniors. For the six years he lived there, I visited him regularly. We would talk about when he would sing us silly songs when we were kids and look at old family photos or play games together on my phone. It was early 2017 when his health declined. He had difficulty eating. Even after the support workers pureed his food, he couldn't get it down. Did you know you can get pneumonia if you can't properly swallow food? He was ninety-four years old the second time he went to the hospital with pneumonia.[72] I remember asking my uncle and aunt what would happen if Grandpa didn't recover. The question hung in the air, unanswered. My uncle shifted, mumbled something about not knowing; his wife tried to change the subject. Death was in arm's reach, but we were like those three monkeys: not seeing it, not hearing it, and definitely not speaking of it.

My family's silence was born from cultural superstitions about death. In Cantonese, the number four sounds like the word for *death*, so we would avoid living somewhere with four in the address. The words for *gifting clock* sound like attending a funeral, so giving someone a watch as a gift was forbidden, even if it was a Rolex. I guess it's not surprising my family wasn't comfortable talking about death, let alone have a plan for it. As the oldest son of the family, my uncle was responsible for making decisions on behalf of our grandpa. I felt worried for my uncle because without any clear directions and having never talked about it as a family, how could anyone make such critical life and death decisions.

Grandpa's second visit to the hospital would be his last. We hoped that he would recover again. His spirits were high even though he wasn't able to eat and continued to physically deteriorate, but the hospital recommended they transfer him back to the seniors' home to die.[73]

---

[72] Needs of the Dying #7
[73] Needs of the Dying #6

Our entire family gathered by him that afternoon in the seniors' home, but when a nurse told us that it could take days or even weeks before he would die, slowly, aunts, uncles, cousins, and my mom started to leave, promising to come back later that evening or tomorrow. I couldn't leave. Something, maybe fear, made me stay. I didn't know how to process what I was feeling. I had questions about what the days ahead would look like, but I could only partially form them in my mind.

One of my grandpa's personal support workers could see my confusion and kindly explained that my grandpa was dying, pointing out the changes in his breathing and the color of his feet. I was scared and didn't know what to do; this was my first time being with someone who was dying. She gently told me to just be by his side, speak to him, and hold his hands. I told my grandpa how much I loved him, that our family loved him, that he was loved, and that everything was okay.

I repeated those words over and over. Sunlight streaming into his room, he looked up at the sun and smiled calmly as he drew his final breath. It was such a powerful moment to see my grandpa in such peace that tears began streaming down my face. I held my grandpa's hand as I cried, overwhelmed with sadness but also relief, love, and amazement. These emotions filled the room: they filled the space left by my family's absence.

Seeing my grandpa die opened my eyes to the complexities of caring for loved ones during the end-of-life process. It inspired me to become an end-of-life practitioner and prepared me to care for my younger brother when his health deteriorated, and he wanted to die. Within four months after our grandpa died, my brother began to ask to end his suffering by suicide.[74]

My brother Torrance loves Harry Potter, My Neighbour Totoro, a popular Japanese anime, and eating french fries. He was born with Duchenne Muscular Dystrophy (DMD). It is a degenerative condition that deteriorates muscles throughout the body over time. He started to have difficulties walking at the age of four and was diagnosed at six years old. He was thirty years old when he said he wanted to die by suicide. That made me take immediate action given our family has a history of deaths by suicide; our grandma and an uncle had both died by suicide less than two decades before.

In late 2015, Torrance had a traumatic experience while testing a new BiPap machine mask, which is meant to help regulate his breathing during sleep. This incident caused him to be anxious throughout the day, feeling like he couldn't control his breath. The anxiety spiraled into fear—fear of not breathing, fear of choking while eating and drinking, fear of not being able to use the bathroom, and fear of losing weight at a rapid pace.

At first, our family was in denial, saying that he'll "shake off" the anxiety and that his breathing will return to normal. But after a year-and-a-half, it was clear he had not shaken it off. The breathing had worsened, and his anxiety of the fears heightened. When I spoke to our mom and her partner about his anxiousness and drastic physical changes, they repeatedly said he'll be fine. Their reaction made me wonder if this was another case of our family's unwillingness to speak about death.

---

[74] Needs of the Dying #10

From my experience with my grandpa, here are four key lessons that I applied to my brother's experience. They are Communicate, Understand, Prepare, and Support (CUPS). As end-of-life practitioners and family caregivers, we need to remember to fill our cups to better support and serve our loved ones and clients.

1. **Communicate**

I had to create the space and opportunity to speak about dying and death with our family and friends. Since this can be an uncomfortable topic, I needed to practice patience and kindness.

When my brother's health started to decline, our family had to face reality and speak about and plan for his death. It was visibly uncomfortable for our mom and her partner. I reminded them that it is valuable for us to listen to him and for us to talk about this together. Hearing his wishes allowed all of us to address the elephant in the room.[75]

Talking about death and dying with loved ones, developing an open and transparent communication channel with the professional health care team—doctors, nurses, care coordinators, personal support workers, therapists, and the personal care team—and including other family, friends, and neighbors can help ensure that everyone is on the same page regarding the person at the center receiving care needs.[76]

Coordinating the communication is a demanding role. I took that on to support my brother. This resulted in improving

---

[75] Needs of the Dying #5
[76] Needs of the Dying #6

care for his changing needs and rallying love and support for my brother and our family.

For the cup of communication, remember to be transparent, patient, and kind with everyone involved, including yourself.

2. **Understand**

When our loved ones or clients express the fears and pain of their suffering, this is an opportunity for us to fill our cup of understanding by being curious. Ask questions to understand what's causing the person's fears and pain. Be aware of when you project your own fears and beliefs.[77]

I didn't fully understand my brother's anxiety because he wasn't able to clearly explain them to us at the beginning. I would ask about his thoughts on death. I assumed he was afraid of dying, but rather it was my own fears of his death.

As Torrance's condition continued to decline, he asked to start the process for medical assistance in dying (MAID). My initial emotional reaction was a clear no. Yet my logical reaction was that my brother, as an adult, had every right to decide what he wanted.[78] I chose not to help coordinate the MAID process for my brother because I struggled with feeling like I would be responsible for killing him if I managed the process.

In the meeting with his palliative care nurse to

---

[77] Needs of the Dying #11
[78] Needs of the Dying #5

understand the MAID process,[79] she explained he needed to complete a lengthy form, have it signed by two non-family witnesses, and confirmed by two doctors who were willing to assess him. This was to ensure that all the criteria were met before the procedure can take place. After understanding the process, my brother decided that he was ready to begin. Hearing the news, my mom and I cried together.

My brother reached out to his family physician to see if he was willing to conduct the MAID assessment. He quickly declined. The palliative care nurse reassured him that if the family physician refuses, they will contact other physicians who consented to the MAID assessments and procedures.

His friends were hesitant to sign as witnesses but later agreed and signed it on his birthday while he was still in the intensive care unit (ICU).

By being curious and practicing patience, he eventually was able to articulate his fears to me. His inability to control his breathing was the cause of his fears. With that understanding, we were able to work with his care team to manage and minimize his pain and suffering.

We also need to understand our family and client's cultural, familial, and religious beliefs on death and dying and hearing my brother's decision for MAID triggered many people in our family. This was because of our family's history with suicide. I had to create space for those family members so that they could speak about their feelings and thoughts about my brother's decision and their traumas of what had happened in

---

[79] Needs of the Dying #8

our family. This was also very healing for me to hear family members openly speak about the deaths of our loved ones.

How full is your cup of understanding? We can better support the person and those around them by being curious about their fears, pains, and beliefs.

3. Prepare

One way to prepare with our loved ones and clients is to ensure an advance care plan is in place. The plan is a valuable guide for family members and the professional care team. It reduces the pressure on a family member or substitute decision-maker (SDM) to make critical decisions during stressful moments. However, recognize that not everyone would be comfortable in preparing.

When our family started an advance care plan with my brother,[80] [81] our mom and her partner were extremely uncomfortable. As we went through each question with my brother,[82] I could see our mom and her partner squirming. Recognizing their discomfort, I reminded them why this was important and encouraged them to ask questions.

Planning can also include completing a will, selecting a Power of Attorney, making funeral and celebration of life arrangements, and any other post-death wishes. I recognized that since taking on the role of an advocate for my brother, I would be the one making any medical decisions during difficult

---

[80] Needs of the Dying #4
[81] Needs of the Dying #8
[82] Needs of the Dying #5

moments. And from the experience of what my uncle had to do for our grandpa, I decided to speak with my brother regularly about his end-of-life and post-death wishes. Completing the advance care plan with him gave me peace of mind and ensured our family was on the same page.[83]

To know what our loved ones and clients want during the end of life and after death fills our cups of preparation.

4. Support

The end-of-life process can be a stressful and emotional one. That's why having a network of support is very valuable. As end-of-life practitioners, we are part of the support network for the family. Other people that the family can rely on include palliative care doctors, nurses, and other health care workers who may be actively supporting the person who is dying.

It was suggested to me at a death cafe, an informal group that meets to discuss death and dying, that I request palliative care support for my brother through the local health network. The palliative care nurse assigned was invaluable. She spoke to my brother and our family about pain and symptom management, what was important to my brother, and his quality of life goals. She spoke with him about the MAID process and reassured us that when his condition changed, they would be able to increase the support for him and our family.

Family, friends, and neighbors are also valuable sources of support. In my brother's case, even though he wasn't able to eat much, we came up with his dream list of foods and shared

---

[83] Needs of the Dying #5

this list with our family and friends so when they visited, each person could bring items from the list, offering my brother something he could be excited about.

People want to help. As practitioners and family caregivers, we need to be clear on what help is needed that can be shared with others who are ready and willing.[84]

And we can't forget about emotional and psychological support. What I heavily relied on was a weekly men's support group. It provided me a safe space to talk and release the emotions I held onto.

What will you do to fill your cup of support? Asking for help from health care professionals, family and friends are ways to start.

As you prepare for or are in the midst of supporting someone that is dying, whether as an end-of-life practitioner or family caregiver, remember to fill your CUPS of Communicate, Understand, Prepare and Support.

~ ~ ~

---

[84] Needs of the Dying #3

The Japanese writer Haruki Murakami says, "Death is not the opposite of life, but a part of it."

This quote reminds me of my first experience with watching a public cremation and speaking about death openly with a friend who took me to the public crematory in Kathmandu, Nepal, in 2016. Together, we watched several ceremonies where groups of family and friends brought the body of their loved one wrapped in a simple white cloth to the Bagmati River to bless the body before cremation.

My friend told me of his first visit to this site to witness the ceremonies and that we bring nothing with us but those that carry us to the river in death. That realization changed the trajectory of his life from focusing solely on running a business to make money to make a difference in his community by opening an orphanage.

What inspires me about this quote is that when we accept that death is part of life, it can help us realize what is most important to living life.

෩ ෬

What was taboo

Talking and preparing for death and medical assistance in dying (MAID) with family and friends was taboo. In particular, MAID triggered a lot of trauma within our family as my grandma and uncle had died by suicide two decades ago. There is a lot of shame and stigma in the Chinese culture around mental health and suicide. As a family, we never spoke about their deaths openly, and family members even lied about their deaths.

Resources I tapped into

- One particular personal support worker (PSW) at the seniors home supported my grandpa for years; her experience and kindness guided me through my grandpa's death.
- A death cafe meetup hosted by a funeral director and end-of-life doula was something I found online and attended to ensure my brother receives the best care at home. I learned from a nurse that was there to request palliative care services through the Local Health Integration Network (LHIN). Hospice Toronto training provided me with practical information and training to apply in caring for my brother.
- Mental Health First Aid, safeTALK, and Applied Suicide Intervention Skills Training (ASIST) are three additional programs I took to better support my brother's mental health and suicidal ideation.
- A palliative care nurse from LHIN was extremely valuable in providing information and guidance on pain, symptom management, and medical assistance in dying.
- Attending a weekly men's support group gave me the space to talk out what I was experiencing and release all the emotions I was experiencing in caregiving. The wisdom of the group also gave me insight and strength to keep moving forward.

- My circle of high school friends gave me the space to grieve and be heard.
- The Universe, my ancestors, and spirit guides in my prayers to them gave me the reassurance and guidance I needed.

Moment of revelation

How peaceful and powerful the dying process can be was a moment of revelation for me.

Self-care tips that helped me

Talking about what I was experiencing with anyone and everyone that I encountered helped me. Being able to share what our family and I were going through was healing and opened up opportunities for support. I participated in two speaking competitions during that time to share my story publicly.

Attending the weekly men's support group allowed me to share my challenges, be challenged on my thought patterns, and be supported during my emotional release of crying and screaming.

Being able to move my emotions and not holding them in also proved helpful. Emotions are energy in motion. When I felt like crying, I did, and when I felt like screaming, I did.

Tips for practitioners

It's okay to say you don't know instead of giving information that may misinform the individual and family.

The impact on me about this experience

- All the training and caregiving experience has led me to complete the end-of-life care doula program.
- I completed my family's and my advance care plans, wills, power of attorney documents, and obtained funeral insurance.
- Learning how powerful and healing it can be for us to speak openly about death and dying.

What I wish I had known when I began on this journey as a practitioner in end-of-life care and what I discovered about it

Realizing how much resources, support, and services are available to the person dying and the family.

ಐ ಆ

Terrence Ho

Terrence is a son, brother, and caregiver. He has held roles in the public, private and non-profit sectors, where he has learned to advocate tirelessly for the greater good strategist, facilitator, and community builder. One of his biggest influences is his younger brother, who lives with Duchenne Muscular Dystrophy. Caring for his brother for almost thirty years has helped Terrence appreciate the unique needs of patients and their caregivers.

Terrence has been inspired by these life experiences to become a change agent and advocate for accessibility, inclusion, and mental health. When he's not advocating for others and caregiving, you'll find him enjoying a podcast or jumping on his trampoline.

Contact Terrence Ho:

Website: www.terrenceho.com
Email: iam@terrenceho.com
Twitter: https://twitter.com/terrencewkho
Instagram: https://www.instagram.com/terrenceho/
LinkedIn: https://www.linkedin.com/in/terrenceho/

Book Recommended by Terrence Ho

Being Mortal: Medicine and What Matters in the End
by Atul Gawande (2017)

I was searching for insights to better support my brother Torrance as we were preparing for his end-of-life care. In the book, Atul Gawande, a practicing surgeon, struggled with supporting his father's end-of-life care. This normalized my experience reading about a healthcare professional struggling in caring for a loved one at their end of life. The nugget I got was around identifying the quality of life measures for the person. This helped me formulate conversations with my brother to identify his quality of life measures. With this information, the care team was able to make better decisions for his care.

About the Book

"Medicine has triumphed in modern times, transforming the dangers of childbirth, injury, and disease from harrowing to manageable. But when it comes to the inescapable realities of aging and death, what medicine can do often runs counter to what it should.

Through eye-opening research and gripping stories of his own patients and family, Gawande reveals the suffering this dynamic has produced. Nursing homes, devoted above all to safety, battle with residents over the food they are allowed to eat and the choices they are allowed to make. Doctors, uncomfortable discussing patients' anxieties about death, fall back on false hopes and treatments that are actually shortening lives instead of improving them.

In his bestselling books, Atul Gawande, a practicing surgeon, has fearlessly revealed the struggles of his profession. Now he examines its ultimate limitations and failures-in his own practices as well as others'-as life draws to a close. Riveting, honest, and humane, Being Mortal shows how the ultimate goal is not a good death but a good life-all the way to the very end." ~ Amazon

CHAPTER 10

COURAGEOUS PLANNING

"It is well, With my soul."

~ Horatio Spafford, Hymnist

"There are a couple of types of ventilation," my doctor explained to me. "And, have you considered some measures of life-saving treatment you're willing to accept?"

We were discussing my request to have a Do Not Resuscitate (DNR) order[85] in my medical chart. I also made it clear that should I ever be diagnosed with a life-limiting illness, I would be seeking medical assistance in dying (MAID).

I'm not sick, and I haven't been diagnosed with a terminal illness. And I'm relatively young, in my mid-fifties. I do, however, want to have as many ducks in order regarding end-of-life care and my wishes clearly known[86] should I be unable to communicate in a medical crisis. I want my dying wishes to be clear and known and supported adequately enough—documented even—so there will be no question should or when ultimately my time comes. And with COVID, I damn well want to make sure I have things communicated, documented, *now* while I am healthy and clear-minded. A bus could hit me, or a car accident could do me in, but COVID brings death more possibly a reality.

My grandmother hadn't discussed her dying wishes for end-of-life care with me.[87] She had discussed things *around* death but not the actual dying part of end of life. We had talked about her funeral, favorite songs, funeral dress, officiant, and not being cremated—those things, but not her medical care at the end.

Her decline seemed fairly rapid from the time of diagnosis to her death, now almost a decade ago. She'd been in long-term care for five years, and once back in her private room after several weeks in hospital, after a few days, she chose to stop eating and drinking. At the time, I didn't realize that what she was doing was voluntary suicide.

---

[85] Needs of the Dying #1
[86] Needs of the Dying #4
[87] Needs of the Dying #14

My grandmother's was my first bedside vigil.

The days were a mix of happy and sad emotions, and once she settled into a persistent sleep, reflective. Reflective of all the times we had shared and lessons I had learned from her. We shared a special bond, one that I know others were jealous of.

Sitting on her bed, looking out the window through the partially open drapes one visit, I just stared. I was in a type of trance, staring out at the sunny sky and gardens, and although the day felt dark and dreary, I was trying to find comfort *out there*, outside. I was seeking comfort or a sign of some sort, away from the sadness inside, hesitating to come back to the room visually because maybe when I turned around, she'd have gone, and I didn't want her to be gone. But maybe I would see a sign outside the window, outside this very still quiet room, a sign indicating to me that she had gone. That's what I had hoped—a sign.

We were no longer talking. She had given her forgiveness and release upon my asking a day or two earlier if there was anything we needed to discuss. I was asking if "we were good." "Of course we are," she gently told me. I felt relief and overwhelm at the same time. Relieved there wasn't anything holding her back from death because she needed an apology from me and overwhelmed because she wasn't waiting for me to say something and could go.

She didn't go, though. There was still time, and sitting, and praying, and waiting, and final visits.

At one point between my visits and going home to rest, I had stopped at our local hospice center to ask to speak with someone who would tell me what to expect and answer my questions about end of life and death. I didn't know how soon or long her death would be but knew it would be. I needed knowledge. A hospice nurse spoke with me for a few minutes, generous because I hadn't booked an appointment, having just dropped in. I asked some questions, teared up and cried, and eventually thanked her for her time. She handed me a little booklet explaining the physical and emotional aspects of the end of life. It was the only information I had.

My mother wasn't talking about it—the dying process. And, she was having none of this "family meeting stuff" that you hear some families have with the doctor and care team. It seemed taboo to ask her about anything now. She had her own stuff going on around her mother's death. My grandmother's death would make my mother the matriarch on our side of the family. She would be alone in her generation as everyone else had died: her father, siblings, aunts, and uncles. And now, her mother. The long-term care team wasn't talking about "it"—the dying process. They were kind and compassionate, but no one asked me if I had questions or needed to talk. I wish they had. I wish someone had.

I wanted and needed to know how long my grandmother would continue to decline as she lay there seemingly asleep. My mother insisted we put cool, damp facecloths on her forehead. I wanted to know how long she would continue to live without taking nourishment? Would she die on her birthday? Before? Or perhaps on her husband's, my grandfather's birthday, the day after hers? How long would she wait?

We had been taught to see death as going on towards our heavenly home, to be gathered again with our loved ones in eternity—church stuff. I was relying on these teachings to help my grandmother find peace in death. I hung onto those teachings to help me feel the pain of this loss just a little less.

Why is she waiting? I wondered. She could go and be released from this body filling with cancer. She could go and be with family on the other side, and yet, another day came.

It seemed all hush-hush as if I were supposed to somehow *know* what was going on through this, her dying process. There were no hallucinations, no physical drama that I noticed. She simply seemed to be asleep.

Eventually, there was a sign. After my husband visited, promising her that he would take care of me, I drove him home, and upon my return trip, midway, I experienced a feeling of lightness as if something had shifted and lifted. It was strange. Ethereal and not something I had ever felt before. Getting off of the elevator at the long-term care home, I saw my mother sitting in the common area, and I knew.

My grandmother died two days after her eighty-ninth birthday. "In her 90th year," her obituary read.

~ ~ ~

As a certified end-of-life hypnosis specialist and doula, I believe it is crucial that we as professionals "walk the talk." Having completed our own work allows us more understanding of what our clients are working through as they complete their documents and discussions.

- My own advance care plan is done and communicated with those family and friends who matter.
- My letter to the medical team who will care for me is written, even though I do not know who that team will include.
- My letter to my spouse is written.
- Will, life insurance policies, financial, and other legal documents are up to date.
- Computer subscriptions and passwords are well documented.
- My power of attorney is chosen, documented, and consulted with fully. My family knows who it is and where my disability and death binder with all my wishes is stored.
- I have chosen an end-of-life doula, and they have been introduced to my power of attorney.
- Even my obituary and social media farewells have been written.

And now, my family physician knows my end-of-life care wishes and has them documented in my medical record.

With all this in place, I can go on living secure, as much as anyone can be, in the knowledge that I have planned well enough for that day when death will be immediately before me.

Yes, I have courageously planned ahead.

~ ~ ~

The Specialty of End-of-Life Hypnosis

Along with palliative care specialists, critical to end-of-life care, there is a relatively new approach to supplementing integrative health care that deserves mentioning: hypnosis, which encompasses holistic and clinical aspects.

I was delighted when I read the following review article "Clinical hypnosis for palliative care in severe chronic diseases: a review and the procedures for relieving physical, psychological and spiritual symptoms."

> In recent years, the scientific study of human consciousness and clinical hypnosis has been transformed from a psychological field, into a neuroscientific topic of research. At the level of brain mechanisms, the consciousness science now synthesizes results from a broad range of techniques for the study of clinical hypnosis. They include electrophysiology, functional magnetic resonance imaging (fMRI), magneto/electroencephalography (M/EEG), and computational models (5-8,12,13). Imaging brain studies have shown that hypnosis influences all of the cortical areas and neurophysiological processes that underlie pain and emotions." (*Annals of Palliative Medicine*, Vol 5, No 4 (October 2016))

When supporting clients with a terminal illness or at the very end of life, as certified end-of-life hypnosis specialists know, better pain management and increased quality of life, including a sense of peace, are possible. These client experiences are supported in the findings of the article noted above:

> Two primary effects of the treatment with clinical hypnosis have been noted: (i) A reductions in daily background pain

and symptoms intensity for many patients; (ii) An increased quality of life and ability to use self-hypnosis, to experience a state of peace, serenity and wellbeing with the reductions in pain and symptoms that can last for several hours, days or months.

Hypnosis itself has been around for centuries: Egyptians in 1550 BC and Mesmer in 1770, Mozart composed the opera "Cosi fan Tutte" while hypnotized, Albert Einstein's theory of relativity was born during self-hypnosis, Tiger Woods uses hypnosis to help keep him focused on and off the golf course, and other fans of hypnosis include celebrities Julia Roberts, Jackie Kennedy, Matt Damon, Ellen DeGeneres, and Oprah.

Many are familiar with stage hypnosis or for quitting smoking. The difference between **stage** hypnosis and **holistic** or **clinical** hypnosis are the suggestions given. Stage hypnosis implies the hypnotist has all the power when, in reality, the client is in control of their actions.

End-of-life choices and medical decisions have complex psychological and social components and consequences; these decisions are often stressful and have a significant impact on suffering and the quality of living and dying. Hypnosis offers a way to move forward with less stress and with a positive impact on one's existence. End-of-life hypnosis offers an exceptionally focused, unique supportive care approach. It can be a powerful complementary therapy for individuals nearing end-of-life. While not a cure for any disease or illness, it addresses the mind-body concerns of the dying in a non-medical and holistic manner.

Seven Benefits of End-of-Life Hypnosis

1. Not Dying Alone – Feeling more connected to others and to a greater sense of spiritual presence is possible by exploring one's inner peaceful aspirations.

2. Reducing Pain or Discomfort – Complementing medications, hypnosis can help one become more comfortable by helping one hypnotically regulate how one feels about pain or other discomforts.

3. Lowering Excess Anxiety or Improving Sleep – Learning the skill of self-hypnosis, more powerful and quicker than meditation with growing scientific support for this mind-body therapy (Globe and Mail, 2017), can help one better cope with changes in environment and treatment protocols.

4. Finishing Personal Affairs – There are often outstanding past, present, and even future concerns like conflict, losses, and disappointments, which can be resolved intimately and privately in one's own mind.

5. Accepting Dependence on Others – By cultivating self-worth and self-care, one can gain a sense of control over thoughts, feelings, and sensations.

6. Embracing Acceptance and Peace of Mind – This approach allows for creating a safe space with a qualified practitioner to talk about fear, guilt, and other emotions.

7. Releasing Fear of the Unknown – It is possible to gently explore intimate thoughts and guide one through a death rehearsal to help alleviate fear.

In the book *Let's Talk about Death Over Dinner* by Michael Hebb, one of the questions posed is, "If you had only thirty days to live, how would you spend them?" Death need not be viewed as fearful or scary. When you consider how you wish to live the moments leading into your own end-of-life transition, you can choose to live joyously and know even in an awful moment, you can be okay. When it's not possible to tell people everything you need or want to for a peaceful end-of-life transition, you can do so in the embrace of hypnosis—non-invasive, gentle, and safe.

You may already be familiar and experienced with meditation. Hypnosis and meditation, in my experience, are like cousins. The main difference is that the meditation is self-induced and with full self-awareness. In contrast, hypnosis is usually induced by another person (unless it is self-hypnosis which is self-induced), and the recipient is in a state of trance. A qualified, experienced hypnosis practitioner acts as a guide and will also teach you self-hypnosis as part of the experience.

Mind-body medicine is on the verge of transforming modern healthcare. During the last thirty years, scientists have begun to explore the interconnections between mind and body and how these are linked to our innate healing capabilities. As this evolution occurs, mind-body modalities will secure their place among the many complementary therapies that can be effective for health maintenance and healing.

A recent study using F-MRIs shows brain activity changes when the patient is experiencing hypnosis. These brain changes are found in the dorsal anterior cingulate, part of the brain's salience network, the dorsolateral prefrontal cortex, and the insula. John Gruzelier, a psychologist and researcher at Imperial College in

London, has been studying hypnosis. "Gruzelier's work is showing for sure that the brain is doing quite different things under hypnosis than in normal everyday existence." There are numerous other studies about the positive impact of hypnosis, easily available on PubMed.

Hypnosis is based on the trance state. We all go in and out of trance several times a day. Think of the last time you stared out a window and daydreamed. That was a state of trance. Or think about watching a movie or reading a book, and time seemed to have flown by. That was a state of trance.

Moving on from the science of hypnosis, which could be a whole chapter in itself, psychologist Charles Garfield in his book *Our Wisdom Years*, encourages us to "find answers for ourselves to ease our anxiety about dying." We can do this in a variety of ways, and one of them can be through hypnosis.

Having some anxiety about death is entirely normal and common. However, for some people, thinking about their own death or the process of dying can cause intense anxiety and fear and is referred to as thanatophobia. It is possible to gently explore intimate thoughts and guide someone through a **death rehearsal** to help alleviate fear. When I was studying and certifying as an end-of-life hypnosis specialist, my husband volunteered for my homework assignments. His belief about what happens after death differs from mine, and we agreed to disagree. I believe there is a life after death for me, whatever that is; it has shifted through my years here on this earth, but that belief still exists. My husband's perspective, believing in good, tolerance, and caring for others, says when his death comes, his candle extinguishes, and that's it.

I needed a test subject for my training homework—a death rehearsal—and he agreed. After the death rehearsal hypnosis experience, he had a shift in perspective. I don't know exactly what he envisioned or experienced, only what he was able to put into words, but it was profound for him in a positive way. It seemed peace-inspiring. As a result, his life tolerance in general has shifted to a softer, gentler, perhaps accepting way.

The next common end-of-life hypnosis session I deliver is centered around **finishing personal affairs.** There are often outstanding past, present, and even future concerns like conflict, losses, and disappointments, which can be resolved intimately and privately in one's mind. In a session focused on **embracing acceptance and peace of mind**, this approach allows for creating a safe space with a qualified practitioner to talk about fear, guilt, and other emotions.

Let's now talk about hypnosis for the caregiver. Hypnosis is a technique to get the client to tap into their subconscious and use their inner strengths to deal with the challenging issue or concern they are presenting. The client is always in control and won't do or say anything he or she doesn't want to. Using the power of suggestion and trance states, hypnosis delves into the deepest levels of the mind. The result: improved behavioral habits and management or supportive therapy of a wide variety of health conditions.

Hypnosis can benefit many psychological and physical disorders, including habit control, weight management, pain control, reactions to stress and anxiety, eliminating phobias, and improving creativity, goal-setting, sleep, and motivation. In addition, it is often used for numerous other health conditions, including gastrointestinal problems, respiratory conditions, anxiety, and dental-related anxiety or as part of a pain-management protocol. Clients have benefited from hypnosis for physical, emotional, psychological, and spiritual concerns. It's also important to know that hypnosis and self-hypnosis can help you tap into your inner resources for resilience, dealing with stress better, and releasing guilt or shame or anxiety over life issues (past or present) or other concerns.

A hypnosis practitioner is similar to an end-of-life doula in that we act as guides, believing that the client has their own innate strengths and ability to tap into them. Like the end-of-life doula, the hypnosis practitioner aims to listen deeply and provide personalized, nonjudgmental care to promote clients' sense of empowerment. Personalization is critical; sessions and hypnosis experiences are unique to the client. We align with the goals, wishes, and needs of our clients, and we respect their choices. We are acting solely for the benefit and care of the client.

ഔ ര

What was taboo

Throughout the final days for my grandmother, talking about the physical nature of death seemed taboo. My family tended to the end-of-life journey as a business discussion, covering things like who would sit with her during the day and especially at night because we didn't want to leave her alone; what personal support worker (PSW) would we get privately for the night-time and what time would she arrive, did she arrive and leave, etc.; who visited and for how long? With my grandmother's physical care covered so well, I wanted to know more about the physical nature of my grandmother's impending death, specifically *when* she would die and how we would actually know it was the last day.

The resources I tapped into

The resources I recognized at the time included:

- The hospice nurse for me emotionally. I sought her out from within the community because our family was not assigned a hospice worker, social worker, or palliative care lead, at least that I knew about.
- The long-term care team. They were obviously there for my grandmother physically, and yet I guess to some degree for me emotionally, but I didn't really tap into them at the time, thinking they were too busy with other residents.
- My church community. I needed the spiritual connection for both myself and on behalf of my grandmother, who had been a stout church-goer with a strong belief in God.
- My husband. He was there for me as I cried about losing my grandmother, along with my frustration with not knowing things about the end-of-life journey or being able to discuss things with my mother. He had lost his parents years earlier, and along with that experience and his support, he was the shoulder I needed.
- My best friend. She was there for emotional support. She had lost both her parents, her father as a young adolescent and her mother as an adult. She was the other shoulder I needed.
- God. I connected through prayer and nature.

A moment of revelation

A moment of revelation for me was the day I realized why my grandmother stopped eating. I didn't realize it at the time, but many years later came to learn that it could have been she was choosing voluntary suicide.

Self-care tips that helped me

What helped me through those final days included eating, sleeping, bathing. I cried as I needed to, and sobbed, and screamed, and cried some more. I held no shame or guilt in any of the feelings I was feeling or how I expressed them. It felt healthy for me to allow my feelings to come out as they wanted and needed to. Perhaps this resulted from the many years of counseling, therapy, coaching, and my training as a life coach and integrative health professional.

Tips for practitioners

I think if someone had asked me, "What do you need or want to know about what's happening to your grandmother?" that would have been helpful. My tip is *not* to ask in a general way, "What can I do to help?" but be more specific, "What do you need to know about [insert topic]?"

What I wish I had known when I began on this journey as a practitioner in end-of-life care and what I discovered about it

I wish I had known how long it takes to die from stopping nourishment. Approximately, anyway.

The impact on me from this experience

This is multifaceted, but these are the most notable:
- I became an end-of-life doula several years later;
- I prepared my own advance care plan to the very detail before I even knew what an advance care plan was. I've also had the discussion with family, pushing through their discomfort to ensure they know my wishes; and
- I have had the health crisis and end-of-life discussion with my family physician and have my wishes, including a Do Not Resuscitate (DNR) order, included in my medical file. I have also discussed this with family, pushing through their increased discomfort to ensure they know my wishes.

೫೦ ೧೩

How are end-of-life practitioners bold spirits?

The end-of-life practitioner is a bold spirit because as they take on a host of caregiving responsibilities, they face their own thoughts on mortality, what it is to live, and what it is to die a "good death."

And, because the practitioner builds such a deep rapport with the client, there is the potential that the impact of the client's death could be overwhelming for the practitioner. How bold is that to agree to knowingly face grief, loss, and bereavement when you didn't necessarily have to?

How are informal caregivers bold spirits?

They typically put their lives on hold to provide care. In addition to providing care, they manage unsolicited advice, unmet promises to help, and those who impose their agendas or care strategies without fully walking in the shoes of the caregiver for any extended length of time.

How is the person in the active stage of dying a bold spirit?

They are a bold spirit because they have no choice but journey forward into the unknown with no way of undoing whatever actions or inactions they took in life. It is what it is now, and they face it, whether that's consciously or otherwise.

What makes you a bold spirit with respect to end-of-life work?

I am willing to talk about death planning and am willing to be brazen in my approach. I ask questions—lots of questions—to gain clarity and more effective processes, strategies, or support. Answers like, "No, we can't do that" do not satisfy me. I want to figure out *how* we can do something. Shying away from a challenging conversation is not my style or in my nature. Life requires honest, open discussion with actionable steps and accountability. And *now*, not later, because we may only have now.

What's the boldest thing you've done in an end-of-life practitioner role?

When the pandemic drew a massive spotlight on the long-term care issue, I created a draft concept for a solution to the staffing crisis in long-term care and emailed that concept to the

Canadian Prime Minister and his immediate team, the Ontario Premier and his immediate team, local Ministers of Parliament, and some key Canadian journalists.

As an end-of-life practitioner, I want . . .

. . . for people to get their heads out of the sand.

This is multifaceted. This means (i) government at the federal and provincial levels to move key aspects of MAID and long-term care into actions that are immediately beneficial to those affected by the policies that delay best care for them, (ii) the medical community in embracing end-of-life doulas and other holistic services within the care team, and (iii) the average person to do the work in planning for their end-of-life care and having those discussions with those people in their lives who matter.

ಔ ಛ

Tamelynda Lux, CCH, PCC, DipAdEd

With over 30 years of experience, Tamelynda has invested much of her career in supporting individuals as a life coach and then evolved her private practice to include hypnosis for life issues and concerns, end-of-life support, and grief and bereavement coaching/counseling.

Certified in the specialty of End-of-Life Hypnosis and as an End-of-Life Doula, Tamelynda provides non-medical, holistic support and comfort to the dying person and/or their family. She is a Certified End-of-Life Doula, Certified Psychological First Aid (Instructor Level) Canadian Red Cross, and has completed Certified Mental Health First Aid with the Canadian Mental Health Association. Tamelynda is actively involved with the aging population, including as a community member on the board of a non-profit for Alzheimers/dementia and long-term care.

Tamelynda is available for individual or family support or speaking engagements.

Please also reach out if you are interested in joining a *peer mentoring circle* for end-of-life practitioners or caregivers.

www.TamelyndaLux.com
info@TamelyndaLux.com
(519) 670-5219
PO Box 29061, London, Ontario Canada N6K 4L9

Book Recommended by Tamelynda Lux

The Needs of the Dying: A Guide for Bringing Hope, Comfort, and Love to Life's Final Chapter
by David Kessler (2007)

This is the first book anyone entering the world of end-of-life caregiving will benefit from reading. I see the needs of the dying as a foundation on which to build an oath or promise of duty as a caregiver to someone in their final days. It's this simple. Read this book first.

About the Book

"In gentle, compassionate language, The Needs of the Dying helps us through the last chapter of our lives. Author David Kessler has identified key areas of concern: the need to be treated as a living human being, the need for hope, the need to express emotions, the need to participate in care, the need for honesty, the need for spirituality, and the need to be free of physical pain. Examining the physical and emotional experiences of life-challenging illnesses, Kessler provides a vocabulary for family members and for the dying that allows them to communicate with doctors, with hospital staff, and with one another, and—at a time when the right words are exceedingly difficult to find—he helps readers find a way to say good-bye. Using comforting and touching stories, he provides information to help us meet the needs of a loved one at this important time in our lives." ~ Amazon

CHAPTER 11

A MOMENT OF TRUTH

"Courage is not the absence of fear.
Courage is fear walking."

~ Susan David

This caregiving moment stopped me in my tracks many years ago. It was a formative experience, one that took place after I had been a hospice nurse for several years. Those first few years were a steep learning curve of clinical knowledge, communication practices, and emotional intelligence. I was in my element. It was challenging and rewarding work.

People I met would often say things like, "I could never do what you do" . . . "You all are extra-ordinary" . . . "Hospice workers are special people." But I knew in my bones that wasn't true. The work of working at the end of life brings extraordinary moments, and we witness moments that feel special and sacred. However, I was aware that my ability to help navigate the complexities of dying and caregiving was both rooted and fragile.

During a fairly ordinary day shift in April one year, the first patient I needed to see had been admitted the night before, and so I headed to his room to introduce myself. I had read in the admission note that Joe was still a vital man, even though his body was falling apart. In his mid-seventies, he was a retired musician and composer and had been admitted to our Hospice Inpatient Unit because his pain had escalated out of control. Joe and his wife Sandra were still reeling from the recent diagnosis of his abdominal cancer and from the rapid physical deterioration that had followed.

I entered his room, and it struck me how sick he appeared. His skin was a yellowish-gray color, dull and drained of health. His arms were skinny like sticks, out of proportion next to his swollen belly and legs. He told me he was eating less each day and found it hard to get out of bed for more than an hour at a time. But even through this evident fatigue and decline, I saw he had an alert and curious mind. He smiled easily, asked me about myself, and told me a few short stories from his life. His vivid expression was a real contrast to the rest of him. Cancer may have taken its toll on his body, but his eyes were still bright and lively. Later, when I returned to Joe's room to bring him his scheduled pain medicine, although tired, he seemed to want to talk some more.[88]

"It's all happened so fast, and we don't feel prepared," he said. "You know, six months ago, we were touring opera houses in Italy!" He paused. "It's hard for my wife to see me like this. She's never known me to be sick. I was always the one to go-go-go. But this cancer is spreading fast, and I know I don't have much time left. I mean, *look* at me." He gestured towards the lower part of his body.[89]

"Do you talk about these things with Sandra?" I asked.

"Well, we talked around it a bit when we first came into the hospice program. But now she doesn't want to discuss any of it . . . with *anyone*. She says we can't let ourselves give up. Maybe she thinks as long as we don't say the word, it won't happen. So we talk instead about the past; we enjoy the memories. It's what she wants to do."

"What do *you* want to do?" I asked. He didn't answer.

The following day, when I walked into his room, I found Sandra seated at his bedside, holding his hand. She seemed tense, sitting straight up in the cushioned chair. I touched her shoulder and told her I was glad to meet her.

"I've heard good things about you through some of your husband's stories," I remarked. She looked at him tenderly, with a kind of sweet sadness. Her body seemed to relax a bit. She turned

---

[88]Needs of the Dying #4
[89]Needs of the Dying #11

to me and said, "Well, I'd love to hear some of those stories. I learn something new about him all the time! Did he tell you about the first time we met?"

Joe rose faithfully to the occasion. He told me about their meeting in church as teenagers, falling into blissful first love, and then the painful separation as Joe went off to college, and their lives took them in different directions. There had been marriages—and divorces—to other people, years of raising families, fulfilling careers for both of them. Their reunion back in their hometown six years ago held the sparks of those early years but was tempered by fifty years of busy lives lived apart. The warmth and affection between them apparent, they retold the story of that reunion. Sandra, in particular, seemed more at ease and comfortable now.

I started to ask about some of their travels together when Joe interrupted me with a very direct stare and the words, "So, how will I know when it happens?"

I paused for a second, not quite sure where his question was going. Sandra's face froze.

"When what happens?" I asked. Knowing his hesitancy to talk about dying with his wife, I wanted to be sure what he meant.[90]

He tapped his chest and said, "When *this* happens."

"Do you mean when your heart stops beating?"

"Yes," he answered, tapping his chest again. "When this stops beating."

---

[90] Needs of the Dying #8

I took a quick breath in and felt dizzy for a few seconds. Then, looking right at him as I talked, I spoke frankly about the possible changes that his body might go through as cancer progressed, and he got closer to dying.[91] It seemed to take way too long for my mouth to say the word *dying*—like it had an extra syllable, and it hung out there all by itself in the sentence. I felt like protecting Sandra. Wasn't there an easier way to say this?

Don't stop now, I said to myself. *And whatever you do, don't look down.* I continued by explaining that he would likely become weaker and less interested in eating and drinking, and that was a natural part of the dying process. I described the slow withdrawal from the physical world and family and friends, as he would sleep more and talk less. His heart rate might become irregular and weaker. His breathing would change, and then eventually, simply . . . stop. "There are as many ways to die as there are people," I said, "but this pattern of slow letting-go is not unusual."[92]

Sandra was now looking as far away from me as she could, her eyes fixed on some point across the room. Joe was looking straight at me, with complete attention. That one question had completely transformed the atmosphere in the room. The easy flow between the three of us had now changed to a tense and highly charged energy around the bed.

Is this what they need to know? I wondered. I looked at Joe's face. He hadn't broken his direct gaze. *He **wants** to know*, I remember thinking. *Somehow I trust he wants me to say this. For him, for Sandra.* I decided to keep talking.

---

[91] Needs of the Dying #13
[92] Needs of the Dying #8

I told them about the effect of dehydration on the body and how it fits into a natural process of the body slowly shutting down, how people who are dying don't seem to feel hunger and thirst. I described the comfort measures of moistening lips and mouth, gentle massage of the skin, and repositioning people in their beds to keep them from getting stiff and sore. Pointing out the good pain control he now had, I emphasized that we can almost always keep pain—and other symptoms—under control through the end of a person's life.[93]

"Physical pain is only part of the picture," I added. "Some people find that their emotional or spiritual pain is bigger and harder to deal with. We work as a team here to help each of you find the resources that you need to walk through this the best you can."

Deep, thick silence filled the room. "We won't hurry anything, Joe, but we also won't prolong your life," I said finally. "How much time you have left is beyond our knowing. But we're about *living* until you die. Free from pain . . . with peace of mind . . . and with as much dignity as possible. We'll be there for you and Sandra, anyway we can."[94]

I was hoping that my voice sounded even and calm as I spoke. It felt like I was vibrating inside, a kind of high-speed adrenaline rush. I heard my words echoing in my head. It sounded as if I really did know what I was talking about. Why should I have been surprised? This kind of conversation had happened many times before with patients and families. After all, it's a large part of what we *do* in this line of work. Of course, I had never experienced

---

[93] Needs of the Dying #8
[94] Needs of the Dying #6

what I was describing to Joe and Sandra, but I had witnessed patterns in dying patients I had cared for and could speak with *some* authority about the dying process. So why was I trembling inside this time? Why did I feel off-balance, like my feet wouldn't hold me steady? What had unnerved me?

These questions ran through my mind as the three of us remained in silence. We stayed in our places but untethered, falling free-form for another moment. Then Joe turned his gaze from me to his wife. She looked at the floor, then directly at him with an expression of anguish and love. It was a naked moment . . . a moment of truth. Tears streamed down both of their faces. We were no longer falling.

I touched Joe's hand and said, "Did I answer your question? I hope that was helpful."

He turned back to me slowly and said only, "Thank you. Thank you."

I went around the bed to where Sandra was sitting. She kept looking at Joe but reached her hand up to grasp mine very tightly. Holding her hand for a moment, I told them, "I want to give you two some time together. Please call for me if you need anything."[95]

I went down the hall into the quiet meditation room to sit undisturbed for a few minutes before seeing my next patient. I couldn't think clearly, with the tumble of feelings that ran through me—fear, relief, anxiety, gratitude, uncertainty. I pictured myself

---

[95] Needs of the Dying #3

back in that moment of truth with Joe and Sandra. So many things were happening at once. An image came to mind of walking across a high wire over a huge, open space below. What was that about? Then I remembered part of the story in Annie Dillard's book, *Holy the Firm*, something I had read years before I was a hospice nurse. At one point, she wrote about the confidence with which some ministers or priests talk about deeply sacred, holy, or inexplicable things—particularly when speaking about God or to God.

> [They]come at God with an unwarranted air of professionalism, with authority and pomp, as though they knew what they were doing . . . I often think of the set pieces of liturgy as certain words which people have successfully addressed to God without their getting killed. In the high churches they saunter through the liturgy like Mohawks along a strand of scaffolding who have long since forgotten their danger.

In my copy of the book, I had underlined that paragraph and added stars and an arrow next to it to grab my attention anytime I came near the page. At the time, I had not understood why those words were so compelling. But there I was, many years later, standing next to Joe, and he was asking me how he would know when he was dying . . . and I talked myself down my strand of scaffolding like a Mohawk medicine woman. My words of hospice nursing were my liturgy—words and phrases used so often, comfortable and comforting.

The difference was that this time, I walked with great care, holding my breath. I didn't walk casually like the Mohawk men in the story. I half expected God to throw a lightning bolt at my feet and knock me over. And I couldn't forget the danger in that room if I had wanted to. It was like a charged field of electricity around us. These were lives at their most precarious. And I was winging it up there, all alone, arms out for balance, hoping to God to keep my words truthful and my voice uncracked.

Looking back on it, there was more happening that day than the three of us could imagine. It takes particular alchemy to transform a situation, and each of us had an integral part in what unfolded in those moments. Joe had the courage to see and then seize the moment of truth-telling[96] without knowing where it would lead. His curiosity was alive and well. Despite my fear of heights and high wires, I trusted that truth-telling with compassion was a walk I could take. Shaky feet were steadied. I was supported by the presence of Spirit at work through me. For her part, Sandra chose to let go of her fear and see Joe in the *here and now* of his dying. With that release came hope for a different kind of healing between them. We had each been changed by the end of that one conversation.

This work has woven into it times of amazing grace when we stumble unexpectedly into a much larger truth than the one we think we are telling. It keeps us from becoming too comfortable with the mysteries around us in hospice work. And it reminds us that we really are never alone or in danger of falling. Then again, how many times can we accompany people to the edge of life and death and still keep our eyes open? It's natural to want to close them after a while. But in time, we are awakened from this kind of slumber, not lulled, but jostled and jolted—when we least expect it. That's a peculiar thing about grace—we don't know when or how it's going to happen to us. Suddenly the familiar words are shockingly new to our ears, and we hear them as if for the first time.

---

[96] Needs of the Dying #8

Now, I may have seen many people die, but that person in the bed in front of me has never died before. And that person sitting in the chair next to the bed has never lost this person before. In truth, I hope I never forget how to tremble in the face of this.

℘ ☙

What was taboo

The taboo in our culture of *not talking about dying* is so strong that even as an experienced hospice nurse in a hospice facility with patients in their last days or weeks of life, I felt some reticence to answer this man's simple question of how he would know he was dying.

Pushing past that taboo also meant that our conversation would likely stir up pain and grief in this man's wife.

That's its own kind of taboo or cultural etiquette: "Don't tell the truth if someone doesn't want to hear it." Or, "Don't cause upset to others."

What this reminded me is that truth-telling can be filled with love and kindness, and compassion.

Resources I tapped into

First, I drew easily from my knowledge, training, and previous experiences as a hospice nurse. Then I followed what he wanted to know. I trusted that this patient was directing the care he wanted to receive, a core belief of hospice and palliative care.

Lastly, I tapped into both courage and compassion as I navigated the heightened emotions in the room.

Moment of revelation

I think it's what came to me once I had stepped out of the room and caught my breath. There was an intuitive leap to the memory of Annie Dillard's words in *Holy the Firm,* those moments of awe that contain both fear and love, and how I didn't want to fall asleep to the sacred nature of those moments in my work with people in precarious times of their lives.

A self-care tip

Go outside. Connecting with the natural world is good medicine for the heart and soul. Feel the sun. Take a deep breath. Touch the ground. Notice what's growing. Notice what's dying. It's all part of the natural cycle for all living things on the planet.

Tip or strategy to help other caregivers

Have a gratitude practice. In a time of intense caregiving, the losses and struggles may be more apparent. Make time daily to write or say out loud three things you're grateful for. Look for different things each day.

What I wish I had known when I began on this journey as a practitioner in end-of-life care and what I discovered about it

I wish I had understood more about the difference between empathy and compassion, especially in terms of their value in the long run as an end-of-life professional. Although empathy is an important quality for a caregiver, overuse can lead to depletion, compassion fatigue, or burnout. Compassion seems to draw from a deeper well of love and kindness, with a certain detachment from the direct suffering within ourselves and others. Compassionate practices are more likely to fill and sustain us through whatever challenges we're experiencing.

ಏ ಐ

How are end-of-life practitioners bold spirits?

We walk right past the taboo of not talking about death. It's such a strong taboo that it feels like it takes courage to open conversations, use words like dying and death, and ask questions that help other people explore end-of-life.

The other is the boldness around being willing to be with this unique kind of suffering of other people. That is a particular kind of suffering. For the dying person, it is the loss of everything they know and so the level of potentially intense emotions, the repetition, and the compounding of grief, grief, grief, loss, loss, loss . . . that takes a boldness of spirit to want to be in that space with people.

Where the boldness comes in for me especially is in holding to this calling so strong that it pulls us through that potential for compounded grief, that repeated witness to the suffering of others. That's why taking care of ourselves and examining and releasing our own grief is so important because you can lose the edge of that boldness with fatigue or numbing out.

As end-of-life caregivers and practitioners, we're often called courageous, and all other kinds of words like angels, which I don't think is accurate. That's why bold spirit appeals to me because you're speaking to the boldness in all of us. Maybe we don't even name it as bold because we usually say we're in service to others. But it's not this demure, quiet, hovering that some people refer to when they call us "angels." It's bold compassion, I would say.

How are informal caregivers bold spirits?

The family and friend caregivers of the person dying are bold spirits, even though they probably don't always feel very bold. It takes a lot to love one another right up until the end. And afterward.

How is the person in the active stage of dying a bold spirit?

I don't think most dying people see themselves as bold. There's often so much diminishment and fatigue as people die a slow death, which is the most common trajectory for dying. And yet, there is nothing that compares to letting go into the complete unknown. I remember hearing the phrase that "courage is fear walking." So I appreciate the idea that we might walk forward toward our dying with that kind of momentum . . . intentional steps . . . conscious steps. Not knowing what's ahead within the unknowable, but having practiced a more conscious navigation of other losses of a lifetime. And then following the wisdom and love we hopefully learned from moving through those other losses and unknown territory. This idea of practice is meaningful to me.

Throughout our lives, we practice letting go in many different ways as we step into new experiences. And there's nothing that compares to dying. Even if you have a really strong belief system, my experience has been that plenty of people with robust belief systems about what happens after death are still really challenged because they never let themselves feel doubt. As it comes closer, sometimes that doubt takes people to some challenging places.

Think about our human experience and what we may have learned about the preciousness of life we aspire to live life as fully as we can and with an open heart and open mind. Just love it, love everything about life. Then, we're asked to let it all go. That's a bold request on the part of whomever or whatever you imagine as the universal intelligence behind life. It's really a bold request. Love it all as much as you can, and don't hold it tightly because, at any moment, it could be gone. I don't know if that's boldness for the dying person, but the act of letting go, surrendering to whatever you want to call this unknown, seems bold to me.

When you think of a client, a patient, or a family member that you helped at their end-of-life journey, think of one who you would consider a bold spirit and tell me a bit about that.

There was a young woman with young children. She saw her ability to "die well" or "consciously" as her last great act of parenting. So many young parents, especially mothers, struggle to let go and die because they are young, healthy, and have a strong heart, in spite of the disease they're dying from. It's challenging and heart-wrenching to watch a young mother not able to let go of the mothering of her children and knowing that the children were going to be without that mothering. I've seen many people suffer through that experience. So for this young mother to come to the place of understanding that how she died would be part of her legacy for her children—that's a bold spirit.

What makes you a bold spirit with respect to end-of-life work?

After all these years, I still feel the call to help people talk more openly about living and dying. It hasn't diminished, and I'm grateful for that. I don't know that there's anything more beyond that.

What's the boldest thing you've done in an end-of-life practitioner role?

It's fascinating how people come up into my memory that I haven't thought of in a while. I can even see the room that they were in when I cared for them. There was a scared, angry, older woman, with very few family or friends, nobody wanting to care for her. One day as she's getting weaker, she grabbed my hand. I leaned toward her, and as she seized my hand and looked at me, I noticed it wasn't anger; it was fear in her eyes. It was a split-second moment of asking *Do I calm her or do I dare to follow her fear?* I chose to move towards the fear.

I said to her gently, "Do you wonder if you're dying?" I didn't even ask her what she thought was going on. I went on, "Do you know that you're dying?"

She answered, "Am I dying?" to which I replied, "This is what I'm seeing. What do you feel? What do you think?" And it all came spilling out of this angry woman, "No one is telling me, no one is talking to me. I've never done it before. I'm scared. Please help me do this."

In that moment, and again over the many years I've cared for the dying, it felt like, *Don't say it. Don't say it. Don't say it.* I just busted through, "Do you wonder if you're dying?"

I don't know if that's the boldest thing I've done, but on reflection, that seems pretty bold. The taboo is very strong against talking openly about dying. So it takes courage to move beyond the taboo. That's what we do in hospice and palliative care and in end-of-life doula or coaching work. We try to normalize dying. We open conversations. We try to make it safe to be vulnerable and express fears. And yet, even in hospice, even in talking with someone in the last stage of their life, it takes intention and compassionate action to give words to the dying process.

As an end-of-life practitioner, I want to . . .

. . . find creative and innovative ways to open the conversation about dying, to bring in more music and art, poetry, and soul-level expression to the continuing transformation of how we die.

Most people don't really want to hear all that much about death and dying unless they're death nerds like me. (Smile.) It's just so nice to have you ask these questions, to have curiosity about all this.

፠ ෬

Janet Booth, MA, RN, NC-BC

Janet has worked as a Nurse for many years at the intersection of quality of life and end of life, as a Hospice/Palliative Care Nurse, an End-of-Life Coach, and Educator. She serves as faculty for the Conscious Dying Institute and the Integrative Nurse Coach Academy and gives classes and workshops around the country on topics related to opening up the cultural conversation about death, dying, and grief. She is the author of *Re-Imagining the End-of-Life: Self-Development & Reflective Practices for Nurse Coaches*, which was chosen as one of the *American Journal of Nursing's* "Best Books of the Year" for 2019.

Contact information:
Boulder, CO
janetbooth15@gmail.com
livingwellnursecoaching.com
LinkedIn: https://www.linkedin.com/in/janet-booth-3790893a/

Book Recommended by Janet Booth

Holy the Firm
by Annie Dillard (1998)

What inspired me is how she captures these ineffable moments with words. The book came to me in that moment of caregiving because of that situation of things that are so profoundly sacred and holy that we can act a little more casually than is warranted.

About the Book

"From Pulitzer Prize-winning Annie Dillard, a book about the grace, beauty, and terror of the natural world. In the mid-1970s, Annie Dillard spent two years on an island in Puget Sound in a room with a solitary window, a cat, and a spider for company, asking herself questions about memory, time, sacrifice, reality, death, and God. Holy the Firm, the diary-like collection of her thoughts, feelings, and ruminations during this time, is a lyrical gift to any reader who have ever wondered how best to live with grace and wonder in the natural world." ~ Amazon

THE NEEDS OF THE DYING

- The need to be treated as a living human being.
- The need to maintain a sense of hopefulness, however changing its focus may be.
- The need to be cared for by those who can maintain a sense of hopefulness, however changing this may be.
- The need to express feelings and emotions about death in one's own way.
- The need to participate in decisions concerning one's care.
- The need to be cared for by compassionate, sensitive, knowledgeable people.
- The need to continuing medical care, even though the goals may change from "cure" to "comfort" goals.
- The need to have all questions answered honestly and fully.
- The need to seek spirituality.
- The need to be free of physical pain.
- The need to express feelings and emotions about pain in one's own way.
- The need to of children to participate in death.
- The need to understand the process of death.
- The need to die in peace and dignity.
- The need to not to die alone.
- The need to know that sanctity of the body will be respected after death.

The Needs of the Dying: A Guide for Bringing Hope, Comfort, and Love to Life's Final Chapter
by David Kessler (2007)

~ included with permission ~

MORE BOOKS RECOMMENDED

Janet Booth also recommends:

***The Wild Edge of Sorrow: Rituals of Renewal and the Sacred Work of Grief,* by Francis Weller (2015)**
This book is a deep and poetic exploration of the sacred nature of grief and loss. In particular, Weller's insights around the *5 Gates of Grief* illuminate layers of grief many of us don't realize we are carrying as "undigested sorrows."

***Facing Death, Finding Hope: A Guide to the Emotional and Spiritual Care of the Dying,* by Christine Longaker (1997)**
This book gave me an insight that transformed my understanding of living and dying—living fully, healing ourselves, and preparing to die is all the same work. This Buddhist perspective is woven throughout Longaker's wise and compassionate handbook.

***The Handbook for Companioning the Mourner: Eleven Essential Principles,* by Alan D. Wolfelt, Ph.D. (2009)**
This is a short book that is full of compassion and insights. Wolfelt distinguishes between the 'treatment model' of grief counseling and the 'companioning model' of caring for people in grief. It inspires all of us to show up as the healers and caring community members we are at heart.

Gale Gagnier also recommends:

Dandelions Blooming in the Cracks of Sidewalks **by Amiga Lhamo (2019)**
>Amita Lhamo uses her luminous stories to reveal the power of simple human kindness and the profundity of being. Within such places, souls peek through the soft spaces of broken hearts like dandelions blooming in the cracks of sidewalks. No matter which way we turn, we find one garden, one ground—we discover the wonder of any heart.

The Top Five Regrets of the Dying **by Bronnie Ware (2019)**
>Bronnie expresses how significant these regrets are and how we can positively address these issues while we still have the time. *The Top Five Regrets of the Dying* gives hope for a better world. It is a courageous, life-changing book that will leave you feeling more compassionate and inspired to live the life you are truly here to live.

A Beginners Guide to the End: Practical Advice for Living Life and Facing Death by BJ Miller & Shoshona Berger (2020)

Tuesdays with Morrie by Mitch Albom (1992)

Accompanying the Dying by Deanna Cochran, RN (2019)

On Death and Dying by Elizabeth Kubler Ross (2014)

Dying Well by Ira Byock MD (1997)

Gone from My Sight by Barbara Kearney, RN BKbooks.com

Lesley James also recommends:

Dying To Live: Learn To Live A Full Life From YOUR Lived Experiences by C.T.S.S. Christine Dernederlanden C.B.T. (Author), Ashely Santoro (Illustrator) (2020)

Love Your Life to Death by Yvonne Heath (2015)

Grief One Day at a Time: 365 Meditations to Help You Heal After Loss by Alan D. Wolfelt Ph.D. (2016)

Tamelynda Lux also recommends:

Our Wisdom Years: Growing Older with Joy, Fulfillment, Resilience, and No Regrets **by author Charles Garfield Ph.D. (2020)**

This is a book that is difficult to put down. Dr. Charles Garfield shares a life journey that is easy to relate to for me in my mid-fifties and in my attempts to understand and appreciate what my older, more senior family members may be experiencing as they are in their late seventies and eighties. The nine tasks he suggests to transform the struggles of aging give me ideas for improving my own life and encouraging others in my life circle or professional care to respond to aging. His comment, "We learn that we're more than our bodies, part of something much larger than we are, and that love and kindness matter most of all," truly resonates with me and inspires me to see the world in a different, brighter light, even in the darkest of hours.

Olga Nikolajev also recommends:

Talking About Death Won't Kill You by Kathy Kortes-Miller (2018)
This book has inspired me because it focuses on death literacy and how we as a society can take part in shifting how we care for the dying, the dead, and the bereaved. Kathy, who I have had the chance to work with, shares her personal story and provides excellent information and insights into end-of-life care in Canada.

On Death and Dying by Elisabeth Kübler-Ross (2014)
Hard to believe this book is in its fiftieth anniversary edition. This small book was instrumental in my initial studies in death and dying and continues to be a good resource for understanding what end-of-life practitioners need to know about the experiences of those at the end of life.

Die Wise by Stephen Jenkinson (2016)

Tuesdays with Morrie by Mitch Albom (2007)

Siby Varghese also recommends:

A Time to Live: Living with a Life Threatening Illness by Barbara Karnes (1994)

> This small book truly inspired me to go deeper into feelings a person may experience while living with a terminal illness, and it touched my heart when I read about our innate sense which inwardly direct to select our choices for treatment or no treatment and the statement "Disease is one of the ways our spirit chooses to leave the body" was really thought-provoking and I liked this book for its simplicity and being real.

CO-AUTHORS

CONTACT INFORMATION

Booth, Janet – Chapter 11
Boulder, CO
janetbooth15@gmail.com
livingwellnursecoaching.com
LinkedIn: https://www.linkedin.com/in/janet-booth-3790893a/

Gagnier, Gale – Chapter 7
PO Box 134
International Falls, MN 56649
galegagnier1@gmail.com
218.324.0226

Ho, Terrence – Chapter 9
www.terrenceho.com
iam@terrenceho.com
Twitter: https://twitter.com/terrencewkho
Instagram: https://www.instagram.com/terrenceho/
LinkedIn: https://www.linkedin.com/in/terrenceho/

James, Lesley – Chapter 4
Markham, Ontario, Canada
lastwishesconsulting@gmail.com
www.lastwishesconsulting.ca
https://linktr.ee/LastWishesConsulting

Jansen, Ashlee – Chapter 8
akinddeathdoula@gmail.com
250-532-3284
www.deathpositiveash.com

Koppenhoefer, Shannon – Chapter 3
www.artraining.on.ca
shannon@artraining.on.ca

Lombardo, Janice – Chapter 6
www.MyAngelJaniceCEOLD.com
email@MyAngelJaniceCEOLD.com
MyAngelJaniceCEOLD@gmail.com
(440) 494-6263
Facebook: MyAngelJaniceCEOLD
Wickliffe, Ohio 44092 USA

Lux, Tamelynda – Chapter 10
www.TamelyndaLux.com
info@TamelyndaLux.com
(519) 670-5219
PO Box 29061, London, Ontario Canada N6K 4L9
Twitter: tamelyndalux
Instagram: tamelyndalux
LinkedIn: tamelyndalux

Nikolajev, Olga – Chapter 1
www.dyingmatters.ca
613-921-2231
olganikolajev@xplornet.ca

Varghese, Siby – Chapter 5
+1 647-575-7935
sibymv@gmail.com
https://www.linkedin.com/in/siby-mathew-varghese-639435195

Waban, Chrystal – Chapter 2
blackbirdmedicines@gmail.com
www.blackbirdmedicines.ca

A FINAL NOTE
From Tamelynda Lux

This book entered into its final editing phase the weekend of Prince Philip's funeral (The Duke of Edinburgh).

I reflected on the phrase "forced intimacy," which Adrienne Arsenault, senior news correspondent, mentioned about the funeral because of the pandemic. It reminded me of the forced intimacy end of life brings no matter how many people are physically present. It's there through the final days, death itself, funeral, and continues through the grief, loss, and bereavement. We are each forced to be intimate with our thoughts about what is occurring or has occurred, how we feel about it, and what will happen in the future—forced intimacy.

As I was editing what it is to be a bold spirit as an end-of-life practitioner, caregiver, or dying person, the common and resounding response by the co-authors was that as much as we could possibly plan, like The Duke of Edinburgh did his funeral, death takes us into uncharted territory—a new journey that no one can define. But as it begins and ends in Ecclesiasticus 43, 11-26: "Look at the rainbow ... by his word, all things are held together."

The co-authors of this book openly shared their intimate experiences and thoughts, and for that, I am grateful because we can all learn from each other.

MORE ABOUT THIS BOOK

Website: www.CaringForTheDyingBook.com
Email: info@CaringForTheDyingBook.com

Facebook: @BoldSpiritCaringfortheDyingBook

Please leave a review on Amazon
because it can help other practitioners and caregivers decide this is a book for them to read while on their journey of providing end-of-life care. Thank you.

If you are interested in participating as a co-author
in a future Bold Spirit Caring for the Dying book,
please contact us.
info@CaringfortheDyingBook.com

ABOUT BOLD SPIRIT PRESS

Tamelynda Lux, Founder
PO Box 29061 London, Ontario Canada N6K 4L9
(519) 670-5219

www.BoldSpiritPress.com
info@BoldSpiritPress.com

**Are you interested in
sharing an experience and becoming a
co-author in a future book?**

Contact me!

Tamelynda Lux
info@BoldSpiritPress.com

www.ingramcontent.com/pod-product-compliance
Lightning Source LLC
Chambersburg PA
CBHW070421010526
44118CB00014B/1849